HEADLINE

No. 321   FOREIGN POLICY AS

CLINTON AND CONGRESS
THE POLITICS OF FOREIGN POLICY

IVCCD Libraries

MCC B.J. Harrison Library
Marshalltown, Iowa 50158

Cover Design: AGNES KOSTRO $5.95
Cover Photo: BERNARD M. DELGADO

The Author

TERRY L. DEIBEL is a foreign affairs analyst, writer and teacher whose career has combined academic pursuits and government service. He is currently professor of national strategy at the National War College in Washington, D.C. He has taught international affairs at the School of Foreign Service, Georgetown University, and has served in the Office of Management and Budget, Executive Office of the President and the Department of State.

Professor Deibel received his Ph.D. from the Fletcher School of Law and Diplomacy, Tufts University, and has written for many leading newspapers and journals. He is also the author of FPA's HEADLINE SERIES No. 280, "Presidents, Public Opinion and Power: The Nixon, Carter and Reagan Years."

The Foreign Policy Association

The Foreign Policy Association is a private, nonprofit, nonpartisan educational organization. Its purpose is to stimulate wider interest and more effective participation in, and greater understanding of, world affairs among American citizens. Among its activities is the continuous publication, dating from 1935, of the HEADLINE SERIES. The author is responsible for factual accuracy and for the views expressed. FPA itself takes no position on issues of U.S. foreign policy.

HEADLINE SERIES (ISSN 0017-8780) is published four times a year, Spring, Summer, Fall and Winter, by the Foreign Policy Association, Inc., 470 Park Avenue So., New York, NY 10016. Chairman, Dave Williams; President, Noel V. Lateef; Editor in Chief, Karen M. Rohan; Managing Editor, Ann R. Monjo; Associate Editors, Nicholas Barratt and Agnes Kostro. Subscription rates, $20.00 for 4 issues; $35.00 for 8 issues; $50.00 for 12 issues. Single copy price $5.95; double issue $11.25; special issue $10.95. Discount 25% on 10 to 99 copies; 30% on 100 to 499; 35% on 500 and over. Payment must accompany all orders. Postage and handling: $2.50 for first copy; $.50 each additional copy. Second-class postage paid at New York, NY, and additional mailing offices. POSTMASTER: Send address changes to HEADLINE SERIES, Foreign Policy Association, 470 Park Avenue So., New York, NY 10016. Copyright 2000 by Foreign Policy Association, Inc. Design by Agnes Kostro. Printed at Science Press, Ephrata, Pennsylvania. Published Fall 2000.

Library of Congress Catalog Card No. 00-110123
ISBN 0-87124-196-X

Preface

THE LATE 1990s were a time of intense partisanship in the United States, resuming a trend that began 30 years ago in the trauma of the Vietnam War. Though Bill Clinton became the first Democratic President to be reelected in a quarter century, his party lost control of Congress to the Republicans just two years into his Administration. Thereafter the legislative and executive branches clashed on a wide range of foreign policy issues, turning the old maxim that "politics stops at the water's edge" into a quaint relic of a simpler past.

The late 1990s seemed, in fact, to all but eradicate what was left of a proud tradition in the politics of American foreign policy. Bipartisanship had been carefully established after World War II to prevent the kind of damage to America's interests that was wrought before the war by the struggles over neutrality, isolation and intervention. It sprang from the same mo-

3

tivation as the Foreign Policy Association, founded after World War I amidst the bitter partisan stalemate over the League of Nations, in the hope that public education could overcome such wrenching divisions. Bipartisanship worked during much of the cold war to help insulate resistance to the Soviet threat from the vagaries of domestic politics, but by the end of the 1990s the tradition seemed nearly dead. The impeachment and trial of President Clinton, the first since the Civil War era, simply reinforced partisan hostilities between and within the branches of government that were as pervasive and vindictive as any in living memory.

And yet, to see foreign policy outcomes in the late 1990s as purely a result of partisanship obscures as much or more than it explains. After all, President Clinton was a so-called new Democrat who took leave of his party's established positions on many foreign policy issues, and on some of these (particularly trade liberalization) he relied on Republican majorities to pass legislation over the active opposition of his own congressional leadership. At the same time, many of the top policymakers of the Bush Administration (1989–93) could be found lobbying in support of Clinton proposals and against the foreign policy positions taken by Republican leaders on the Hill. Despite all the Republican-Democratic fireworks, then, it is clear that something more than partisanship was going on.

I argue that that something is factionalism, a splitting of each party into two schools of thought about America's role in the world and especially about the means by which that role should be played. Of course, no factional division can explain how all individuals approach every foreign policy issue; positions are influenced by a wide variety of motivations, some philosophical, some practical, some personal, some doubtless electoral. But I believe that today's basic foreign policy split in each political party, the split that underlies positions on many if not most specific issues, is caused by a fundamental collision between the party's domestic mission and the realities of the post-cold-war world. I also believe that those Democratic and Republican dilemmas will not soon be resolved, and that therefore an appreciation of the views of the four factions is critical not only to understanding America's recent past but also to predicting where U.S. foreign policy is likely to go in the early years of the twenty-first century.

What follows is an attempt to define the four factions and to illustrate their views by examining their interaction through the critical foreign policy contests of the Clinton years. Chapter 1 begins by tracing broad developments in American and international politics that set the stage for the factions' birth. It then explains the parties' missions, the dilemmas those missions create in the post-cold-war era, and how those dilemmas divide party members. Chapters 2 and 3 focus on these factions in the Democratic and Republican parties, respectively. No attempt has been made to categorize every member of Congress; instead, conclusions are based on the public positions and key votes of the members who are most active on important foreign policy issues—roughly 30 to 40 members of each party in the House and Senate. Since the story of the late 1990s is essentially the story of the clash of one Democratic faction (represented by the Clinton Administration) against one Republican faction (represented by leading conservative Republicans in Congress), these two groups will receive the most attention, but their counterparts in each party will also be defined and discussed. Finally, Chapter 4 will draw conclusions from the partisan factionalism of the 1990s and attempt to look ahead at what one might expect in the early twenty-first century.

Research on this project has been under way for almost as long as the struggle it documents, and many have helped in bringing the work to fruition. Coincidentally, I first began drawing together my ideas on the policies of the Republicans in Congress in 1996 as a result of an invitation to speak to a League of Women Voters group in Washington, D.C., that was participating in FPA's Great Decisions program. Since then I have had the opportunity to refine my ideas before international visitors sponsored by Meridian International Center and have benefited from participating in the Congress and Foreign Policy project of the Institute for the Study of Diplomacy at

Georgetown University in 1998–99. I would also like to thank specifically Alton Frye, Alan Tonelson, Mary Locke and Ole Holsti for reading and offering specific comments on earlier versions of this manuscript, as well as the National War College for providing the research time necessary to complete it. Of course, the views expressed herein are only my own and do not necessarily represent the positions of the National War College, the National Defense University or any department or agency of government.

Terry L. Deibel
Washington, D.C.
September 15, 2000

American Politics, Political Parties and the Post-Cold-War World

THE FOREIGN POLICY of any country results from two kinds of influences. One is external pressures, the impact of events in the world at large as seen by policymakers at home. The other is internal factors, the interplay of domestic interest groups, partisan politics, economic pressures and the like. While policies primarily influenced by the first have at least a chance of being rational—after all, foreign policy is supposed to be *about* the external environment—policies resulting from the second may be little more than the hobbyhorses of politicians who hope to ride them to power. The forces behind them may have little to do with foreign countries or issues.

Today, of course, there is hardly a shortage of important foreign issues to drive policy, from Third World chaos to terrorist threats, and from a return of Russian totalitarianism to looming Chinese power. But none of today's crises, nor all of them put together, constitute the kind of danger that the United States lived with for almost 50 years during the cold war: the possibility of deliberate annihilation by a hostile, totalitarian regime. Whether or not Americans had a central organizing principle to guide foreign policy during that era, they certainly had a central organizing threat that concentrated the national mind and focused it overseas. But now, with the Soviet Union gone, the balance of influences on American foreign policy has shifted dramatically away from external to internal factors. License has been given to the interplay of domestic interest groups and political agendas in a way that hasn't existed for decades. Hobbyhorses are being ridden everywhere.

The Constitution has been aptly described as an invitation for the branches of government to struggle over the conduct of foreign policy. In this post-cold-war era, as in all postwar eras, the rise of domestic factors is accompanied by the ascendancy of Congress, as the legislature reasserts itself against the power the executive naturally gathers in time of crisis or war. It is therefore impossible to understand the new pattern of American statecraft by looking only at the presidency. The Congress now insists more than ever upon having its say in foreign policy, and its say is more needed as post-cold-war domestic and foreign issues increasingly merge.

Mix of Internal and External Issues

The new pattern of American foreign policy in the post-cold-war era is thus one that mixes internal with external issues far more than in the recent past and one that involves policies generated by Congress almost as much as those championed by the White House. Although the current relationship between the branches may seem dominated by partisanship and personal vindictiveness, a careful look at their foreign policy struggles over the last half of the decade reveals a far more complex, interesting and substantive pattern. Understanding it begins with three linked premises:

First, today's political parties are much more ideologically homogeneous, politically extreme and geographically concentrated than formerly. Over the past 30 years the "big tent" parties of the 1950s and early 1960s have given way to parties that more clearly stand for something and that have definite positions on the political spectrum. Under the leadership first of President Ronald Reagan (R-Calif.) and then of House Speaker Newt Gingrich (R-Ga.), and powered at the local level by the fundamentalist Christian Right, the Republican party lost moderate and progressive leaders like Jacob Javits (N.Y.) and Nelson Rockefeller (N.Y.), gained conservative membership in the Mountain States of the West, and transformed the conservative South from a solid bastion of the Democratic party into a Republican stronghold. For the Democrats, on the other hand, the defection of the South meant a dramatic weakening of the party's conservative element just as the country's growing ethnic and racial diversity was transforming the traditional "melting pot" into a new mosaic. Adding these new groups to its older membership, the Democrats became more than ever a party of liberals on both coasts and in the northeastern quarter of the country, and of women, union members, blacks, immigrants and various disadvantaged groups across society.

Taken together, these changes mean that each party is more cohesive but that there is less common ground between them. On domestic issues, at least, the Democratic party is more and more the party of the Left in American politics, while the Republicans are the party of the Right. Surveys of opinion leaders confirm this tightening correlation between party and ideology. Comparing 1996 data with polls done over the past 20 years, Professor Ole Holsti of Duke University found that "increasing numbers of Republicans (78 percent) identify themselves as conservatives, while Democrats are predominantly on the liberal side (68 percent) of the ideology scale; conservative Democrats (6 percent) and liberal Republicans (4 percent) are a vanishing breed among the rosters of American leaders." In a system where separate institutions share power and must therefore work together to get things done, this polarization means that electoral outcomes putting one party in control of the Congress and another in the White House are far more consequential for governing. Although the country often had government divided by party during the cold war, today it matters more than ever. And while "new Democrats" like Clinton and "compassionate conservatives" like Texas Governor George W. Bush may seek to mitigate this polarization, it seems unlikely that these countertrends will take us back to anything like the Republican party of President Dwight Eisenhower (1953–61) or the Democratic party of John Kennedy (1961–63).

Second, despite, or perhaps because of, its ideological cohesion, each party is divided into two very different factions on foreign policy. For as they have become more ideological, the parties' core values on domestic policy, the beliefs that make people *become* a Democrat or a Republican, have come to matter more. At the same time, party missions based on those values run headlong into uncomfortable realities of the post-cold-war world, posing acute dilemmas for party members. The way members resolve those dilemmas splits each party into two factions on foreign policy, one necessarily more centrist, the other tilting toward the political extreme. It is in the contest between and among those factions, as much as in the contest between the parties or the branches of government, that the new pattern of American statecraft can be found.

Third, the shift of Democratic power from the Congress to the White House in 1992, and of Republican power from the White House to Congress in 1994, matters profoundly. This is so because the faction that defines and expresses the party's foreign policy positions is largely determined by which branch of government the party controls. For reasons buried deep within the Constitution and structure of the U.S. government, Congress tends to be more ideological and extreme in foreign policy, the President more moderate and centrist.

In the first place, of course, elected officials reflect their constituencies. The smaller the electoral district, the more likely it is to contain people with similar opinions, and the greater the possibility that they will elect members whose views are outside the mainstream of the rest of the country. Moreover, since the Constitution gives the President preeminent power to conduct foreign relations, members of Congress know that the White House will usually be blamed (or get credit) for foreign policy results. They therefore feel free to push human rights, slash foreign aid, pass resolutions that outrage foreign governments, demand overseas interventions, impose economic sanctions on scores of countries, or refuse to fund international organizations despite treaty obligations to do so, all with aplomb. The "classic congressional foreign policy maneuver," according to former Representative Lee Hamilton (D-Ind.), is that "we get the domestic political advantage, but the President gets the responsibility."

The President, on the other hand, is elected by the whole nation in all its diversity and therefore is more likely to be a moderate in his policy preferences. Moreover, he will tend to be more cautious and sober in his policy style, knowing that he will be held accountable by the public for policy outcomes. Even more important, a party in the White House is pulled toward the political center by day-to-day contact with real foreign policy problems and the real foreigners who personify them. For these reasons the foreign policy struggle, always more vigorous between the branches of a divided government, will usually be between the moderate faction of the party controlling the White House and the extreme faction of the party controlling the Congress.

These three developments—the changed locus of the Democrats' and Republicans' power within the government; their ideological cohesiveness as parties of the Left and Right; and the development of foreign policy factions within them as their central values collide with new post-cold-war realities—have combined to shape the politics of American foreign policy since the end of the cold war. Based on these premises, a system of partisan factionalism can be seen operating in recent struggles between and within the branches over key foreign policy issues. What follows is a description of its essential characteristics, beginning with the Democrats.

The Democrats: Idealists and Pragmatists

The Democratic party's basic mission, its reason for being, is essentially compassionate in nature. Above all, Democrats want to use government to help the disadvantaged in society, to re-lieve human suffering and uplift the downtrodden. This, at least, is their mission the way Democrats themselves might see it. A cynic—or a Republican—would probably say that what the Democrats are really about is giving people something for nothing, or (as Reagan charges in his memoirs) confiscating the earnings of people who work and redistributing them to people who don't. But Democrats would put it more charitably. They would say that the whole point of their party is to help those who cannot help themselves, a mission that springs not from socialist economic ideology but from the most profound, com-passionate and disinterested moral considerations.

This *raison d'être* has several corollaries, the most important of which have to do with the role of government in the economy. Since government is the major instrument available to redress inequality and relieve human suffering, Democrats tend to have a positive attitude toward government and toward regulation and management by government. Their comfort with government underlies their belief that it can help "grow the economy," as President Clinton often said, meaning at a minimum that the public sector must make certain kinds of investments to encourage economic growth and, at a maximum, that government can make the kind of decisions often grouped under the phrase "industrial policy" better than the unfettered free market. In international economics, the idea that govern-ment is good feeds the affinity in some parts of the Democratic party for protectionism, also a manage-the-economy-via-gov-ernment idea.

When it comes to foreign policy, though, the Democratic party's core mission runs into an immediate problem. There is, unfortunately, a great deal of inequality and suffering in the world. How does one distinguish between the suffering of Americans and foreigners, or between the suffering of one for-eigner and another? It is not at all easy to do so on moral grounds, especially for a nation founded on the proposition that all are created equal. Obviously the United States does not have the wherewithal to deal with the suffering of all humanity, or even a small portion of it; Washington cannot rescue all the destitute even at home. And yet Democrats cannot let go of morality, for it is their sense of morality that enjoins and justifies their party's mission in the first place.

Split within Democratic Party

It is on this dilemma that the deepest, most fundamental foreign policy split within the Democratic party takes place. It is a split between factions one might label *idealists* and *pragmatists*. Idealists solve the dilemma by simply ignoring it. They are explicit about wanting to apply the party's raison d'être overseas, to do whatever can be done to relieve foreign suffering even as the government tries to help those in need at home. Whether there are atrocities in the former Yugoslavia, or a militia rampage in East Timor, or the collapse of United Nations peacekeeping in Sierra Leone, they are ready to use American aid and, if necessary, American armed forces to help. As Secretary of State Madeleine Albright famously put it to General Colin Powell during a debate over intervention in Bosnia, "What's the point of having this superb military that you're always talking about if we can't use it?"

The usual counterpoint to liberal idealism in foreign policy is conservative realism, the idea that not moral principle but power is controlling in international affairs and therefore must be at the heart of foreign policy. But realists today tend to be Republican; there were virtually none in the Clinton Administration's upper ranks and very few Democratic realists in Congress. Instead, the counterpoint in the Democratic party to idealism is *pragmatism*, the idea that principle is only the starting point for effective governing.

Democratic pragmatists do not reject the party's reason for being or even question the desirability, other things being equal, of relieving human suffering overseas. But they are acutely sensitive to the resource and time constraints on the government and its leaders. The budget deficit for fiscal year (FY) 1993, spanning Clinton's first months in office, was $255 billion, and pragmatists recognized that overseas interventions could be costly affairs. More important, they were risky. As the country's experience in Vietnam had demonstrated decades earlier, the United States could get itself mired in foreign adventures that would sap the time, policy energy, public support and financial resources needed to accomplish the domestic program on which Clinton had been elected. Pragmatists simply felt that priorities had to be set, that the Administration should avoid foreign entanglements, even idealist ones, and focus its attention on uplifting the downtrodden at home.

As the label implies, pragmatists are much more willing to compromise in their overall approach to governing than those on the ideological extremes of either Left or Right. Writing in *The Washington Post* even before Clinton took office, Nicholas Lemann pointed to two grand traditions in the Democratic party, the courthouse-square tradition of the South and the progressive tradition spawned in the Northeast and Upper Midwest. Progressives were idealist reformers who worked for such causes as the abolition of child labor, women's suffrage, temperance and prison reform; they took their stand on principle and were loathe to compromise. Democrats in the South, by contrast, learned to govern by conciliating different interests, making deals that might well fall short of the ideal but seemed necessary in the circumstances to get something accomplished. It wasn't that pragmatists lacked the principles of idealists, just that they wouldn't rather be right than effective in implementing their principles. They understood, as the realist Henry Kissinger wrote, that for those in power it was not "enough to be plausible in argument; one had to be convincing in action."

The question in the early years of the new Administration was in which camp the President belonged. A four-term governor of a small southern state whose party's strength was now concentrated in the Northeast, Clinton came to office with little track record in foreign or national security policy. On the one hand, his campaign rhetoric sounded rather idealist: he chided the Bush Administration for its slowness in assisting the birth of democracy in Russia and Eastern Europe, for coddling dictators in China and for ignoring humanitarian atrocities in Bosnia.

On the other hand, his determination to focus on domestic reform meant inevitable competition for the resources that would be needed for idealist schemes abroad. From the outset, the Administration threw itself into massive projects for reform of health insurance and welfare, and Jim Hoagland of *The Washington Post* argued that Clinton had made the cautious Warren Christopher his secretary of state to do damage control in foreign affairs while he concentrated on domestic projects. Only time and concrete policy decisions would reveal where along the idealist-pragmatist spectrum this President would stand.

The Republicans: Unilateralists vs. Internationalists

The Republican party also has a central mission, a core reason for being, that has crystallized as the party has moved to the Right. The Republican mission is to preserve free competition in American society. What Washington should do, Republicans would say, is not to ensure equality of results in that competition but to maintain a level playing field to ensure equality of opportunity as competition plays out. A cynic (or a Democrat) would no doubt put it differently, pointing out that even a level playing field simply ensures that the privileged and powerful will continue to win, that the rich will get richer while the poor get poorer. But Republicans would counter that their party is not about protecting the wealthy and powerful but about arranging things in the public sector so that anyone can compete, so that whoever has energy and talent can succeed in the private pursuits that have always made America great.

When it comes to the value of government and its role in the economy, this mission has nearly opposite corollaries to the Democrats'. Although many GOP governors are activists, Republicans at the national level tend to see government, particularly the federal government, in a negative light. Valued by Democrats as an instrument to redress inequality, government for Republicans is at best a necessary evil that is required for attending to unambiguously public tasks, at worse an obstacle to the free competition they so value—in other words, at least as likely to be part of the problem as part of the solution. As a result, they have wanted to shrink government and government spending as much as possible. In the economy, Republicans favor deregulation and a laissez-faire, largely hands-off role for government, which usually translates in international economics into support for free trade.

For Republicans, international as well as domestic affairs follow the logic of the party's core mission: they are competitions for wealth and power in which Americans should use every means available to prevail. Republicans believe that what syndicated columnist Charles Krauthammer has called the American unipolar moment following the cold war invites this country, the world's sole superpower, to outcompete everyone. And in many cases, perhaps in most, the United States *can* outcompete its international rivals—if it is willing to bear the costs and risks of competition. Unfortunately, however, such costs and risks are growing as nations become more interdependent and economies more globalized. The Republican image of all life as a struggle for survival of the fittest may well be more in tune with the present anarchical world order than the Democrats' concern with principle and morality, but it poses its own dilemmas in a world where cooperative action is becoming more necessary and more in evidence. If Democrats are ill-equipped to deal with the ubiquity of inequality in the world, then, Republicans face the dilemma of how to deal with the growing constraints posed by interdependence and globalism on any nation's unilateral action.

It is on this dilemma that the deepest, most fundamental foreign policy split within the Republican party takes place. It is a split between *unilateralists* and *internationalists*. When the Republicans took control of Congress after the 1994 elections, there was none of the uncertainty regarding their foreign policy views that had attended President Clinton when he came into power. Senators like Jesse Helms (N.C.) and Trent Lott (Miss.) had track records in office, and the 73 Republican freshmen elected to the House that year ran on a conservative platform, the "Contract with America." Not all conservatives, to be sure, are unilateralists; neither Speaker Gingrich (nor his successor

Dennis Hastert (Ill.) share all the foreign policy views of their unilateralist colleagues. But the center of unilateralist Republican policymaking lies with the radical or "movement" conservatives that have dominated the party in the House of Representatives since 1995, and with key conservative leaders of the Republican party in the U.S. Senate.

Counting unilateralists is an imprecise task, but 49 members of the Class of 1994 survived two subsequent elections into the 106th Congress (1999–2000), and one unilateralist estimated the total number of movement conservatives in the House at 60–80 in the 105th Congress (1997–98). They have been important out of all proportion to their numbers because the small and shrinking majority the Republicans held in the House required their leaders to get substantial numbers of them on board if the party was to pass legislation over Democratic objections. In the Senate, by contrast, the unilateralist presence was somewhat weaker, but its influence was magnified because unilateralists held key positions in the majority like the leader-

RALL©Ted Rall. Reprinted with permission of UNIVERSAL PRESS SYNDICATE. All rights reserved.

ship, whip and Foreign Relations Committee chairmanship.

Like their idealist cousins across the aisle, Republican unilateralists solve their party's dilemma by simply ignoring it. They discount interdependence and globalization, deny most of the threats these produce, and are deeply resistant to the growth and use of multilateral agencies. Whereas Democrats tend to be creatures of the public sector and comfortable with government and politics, most Republican conservatives came to Washington from the private sector. They were intensely focused on domestic affairs, and most lacked international experience, military service, or even much foreign travel. Their mandate was to balance the budget and cut the government down to size, and a combination of disinterest in foreign affairs and a belief that the end of the cold war meant the end of any real threat from abroad led them especially to favor cuts in the parts of government dealing with foreign affairs. Moreover, the unilateralists' activism was strengthened by their sense that it was less dangerous for Congress to challenge the President in the post-cold-war environment and fired by their conviction that Clinton's personal conduct rendered him morally unfit to hold the nation's highest office.

The unilateralist approach to foreign policy thus begins with a lack of interest in and knowledge about foreign affairs and with opposition to government in general. Most unilateralists are also strong nationalists, worried about protecting American sovereignty from the effects of globalization and from the very international bodies that the Administration feels are essential to deal with them, just as they want to protect American society from overactive federal government. Their distrust of international instruments and agencies and their intense nationalism often lead to an all-or-nothing approach to statecraft, a tendency to throw America's considerable weight around in the world with a take it or leave it, "in your face," "I won't stand for this" kind of attitude. But mainly unilateralists tend to oppose multilateral, conciliatory efforts—where goals may have to be compromised to achieve a peaceful resolution—in favor of solo American action on maximum American terms.

©The New Yorker Collection 1994 Mick Stevens from cartoonbank.com. All Rights Reserved.

Republican Internationalist Views

As the policies of the Bush Administration and the positions of a few moderate Republicans on the Hill demonstrate, internationalist Republicans have quite a different approach to their party's core dilemma of how to exercise American power in a competitive yet interdependent world. In many respects, to be sure, they agree with their more radically conservative colleagues. Like the unilateralists, Republican internationalists see competition as the major feature of international as well as domestic life, and they too are quite willing to take full advantage in that competition of their country's overwhelming power. But Republican internationalists have a different view than their unilateralist brethren about the importance of foreign affairs. They do not accept the premise that the end of the cold war means the end of any serious threats from abroad, and they reject out of hand the idea that the United States should concentrate on domestic affairs to the exclusion of foreign policy. For internationalists, in fact, the unipolar moment provides the United States with an extraordinary opportunity to shape and manage the international environment in ways that will advance American interests for decades to come. It is an opportunity, they feel, that must not be squandered.

Republican internationalists take a distinctly realist or geo-political approach to what President George H. W. Bush called the new world order, focusing far more on balances of power between countries than on the issues of their internal governance (such as democracy and human rights) that so exercise idealist Democrats. Like Democratic pragmatists, though, Republican internationalists do worry about the costs and risks of foreign involvement; it was President Bush, after all, who told the world in his inaugural address that the post-cold-war United States had "more will than wallet." The central dilemma of all Republicans, that of applying a competitive mission to an increasingly interdependent world, is therefore not one that internationalists can avoid. Their answer can perhaps be called American leadership, a middle ground between the reflexive embrace of multilateralism characteristic of idealist Democrats and the rejection by unilateralist Republicans of all formal international cooperation as ineffective and likely to compromise American sovereignty.

Republican internationalists are concerned about some if not all of the newer transnational threats, and they recognize that international instruments are often the best means for dealing with them. Although they embrace a much narrower definition of the national interest than most Democrats, they believe that international organizations and treaties can sometimes be used to serve those interests at less cost and risk than unilateral action, while their appreciation of America's enormous relative power in today's international system mitigates any concern about the preservation of American sovereignty. Indeed, they are confident that Washington's overwhelming power makes it possible to bend international instruments to its own purposes, and that using them to lower the costs and risks of American action can make it possible to intervene even in instances where the national interest does not justify the much higher expense and greater danger of unilateral action.

The reader should not conclude from this introduction to party factionalism that no characteristics hold Democrats and Republicans together. In general, Democrats tend to support interventions abroad in humanitarian causes and Republicans to oppose them; Republicans tend to support more spending on the military than Democrats; most Republicans support freer trade, while most Democrats are leery of it; most Democrats have a more favorable view of international and multilateral organizations than most Republicans; Democrats tend to favor the more cooperative tools of statecraft and Republicans,

DEMOCRATS		REPUBLICANS	
IDEALISTS	PRAGMATISTS	INTERNATIONALISTS	UNILATERALISTS
LEFT	CENTRIST		RIGHT

the more coercive ones. Still, the very different ways in which members resolve the dilemmas posed when their party's mission runs into the developing realities of the post-cold-war world have created centrist and extremist factions in both parties. And on most issues the centrist factions have more in common with each other than with the extremist factions in their own party, as the diagram above depicts. More surprisingly, on some issues the extreme factions in the two parties find themselves uncomfortably close, even cooperating.

Opinion data gathered from a broad spectrum of American leaders in 1996 confirms the linkages sketched above between views on foreign policy and liberal or conservative positions on domestic issues, and shows that they extend well beyond Congress to media leaders, military and Foreign Service Officers, labor leaders and academic experts. In an analysis based on a scheme created by Eugene R. Wittkopf of Louisiana State University, Holsti first groups American opinion leaders according to whether they favor or oppose two types or "faces" of internationalism: cooperative and militant. Those who favor both are labeled *internationalists* and those who favor neither are *isolationists*, while those who support only cooperative internationalism are *accommodationists* and those who support only militant internationalism are *hard-liners*. He then subdivides these groups into *unilateralists* and *multilateralists*, according to whether they prefer that the United States operate alone or in cooperation with allies and international institutions. Comparing these groups' preferences in foreign policy with their views on domestic issues, he finds that unilateralists, and particularly hard-liners, are typically the most conservative, while multilateralists, especially accommodationists, are usually more liberal. Moreover, the stronger an individual's preferences for unilateral or multilateral action in foreign affairs, the more likely he or she is to be a conservative or a liberal on domestic matters. As among Republicans in Congress, the strongest correlation is between unilateralism and conservatism: among opinion leaders from all walks of life, 89% of strong unilateralists are conservatives.

But this generalized picture of partisan factionalism is only a starting point upon which to build an understanding of the politics of American post-cold-war foreign policy. A more complete grasp of each faction's views can only emerge from a detailed examination of its foreign policy struggles over the key issues that have dominated American statecraft in the late 1990s—the task of Chapters 2 and 3.

2

The Democrats:
Idealists and Pragmatists

THE STRUGGLE BETWEEN idealists and pragmatists for control of the Democrats' foreign policy has not only been waged between the White House and Congress. It was also fought within the Administration itself, particularly during its first two to three years in power. Out of office for a dozen years, the Democrats' last presidency was chiefly remembered for the 1979 Iranian hostage crisis and the Soviet invasion of Afghanistan, hardly the kind of foreign policy experience the Clinton Administration wanted to repeat. In his campaign, the new President had found it easy to criticize President Bush for being mired in the ways of the cold war, but his own principles set no consistent foreign policy direction.

Clinton ran on three so-called pillars: first, restoring American competitiveness in world trade (the foreign policy component of "It's the economy, stupid!"); second, spreading democracy overseas; and third, reforming the American military for post-cold-war tasks. The first pointed to a highly self-interested statecraft more focused on geoeconomics than geopolitics; the second was strongly idealist and implied an altruism that might well compete with the economic thrust of the first; and the third was not an objective at all but rather an approach to refashioning one of the tools of statecraft. What all this meant in practical terms remained very much to be seen.

Once in power, Clinton set off in a strongly idealist direction, or more accurately, in several idealist directions. The Administration championed "assertive multilateralism" as a way to deal with humanitarian problems overseas; it expanded American goals in Somalia, where President Bush had intervened in the last months of his Administration simply to relieve widespread starvation, into an ambitious effort at nation building under UN auspices; it tied most-favored-nation (MFN) treatment of trade with China to Chinese human-rights policies; it pledged to back the 1993 UN-brokered pact negotiated on Governor's Island, New York City, to restore an elected government that had been deposed by a military coup in Haiti; and, in a self-conscious effort to replace cold war "containment" with a new doctrine of "enlargement," it declared the spread of market democracy to be at the center of U.S. foreign policy worldwide.

Role of Idealist Democrats

Among the reasons for these policies was the strong influence of idealist Democrats within the Administration. Idealism, of course, had dominated the prior Democratic Administration (1977–81), springing from the born-again Christian moralism that had led Jimmy Carter to make human rights his signature foreign policy. And most Democrats who had policymaking experience at the outset of the Clinton Administration got it working for Carter, mainly for Secretary of State Cyrus Vance. Clinton's Secretary of State Christopher, his National Security Adviser Anthony Lake and deputy Sandy Berger, and UN Ambassador Albright all cut their foreign policy teeth on the Carter team, as did many lower-level political appointees. In terms of personnel, then, Clinton I was Carter II.

24

But idealist pressure also came from the Hill. The Democrats still controlled Congress in 1993–94, and the idealists who naturally dominated the party there were eager to see policies enacted that had languished in the Reagan and Bush years. They put strong pressure on their President, most notably perhaps when the Congressional Black Caucus pushed an obviously reluctant Administration into action on Haiti.

Whether urged by idealists in the Capitol or in his Administration, however, Clinton's early foreign policies did not go well. Successive American plans to end the civil war in Bosnia were rejected by the Europeans as long as American troops weren't committed alongside their own, so Serbian shells kept falling on Sarajevo, the North Atlantic Treaty Organization (NATO) seemed in disarray, and the Administration appeared indecisive and weak. Then, in October 1993, a firefight in Mogadishu, Somalia, left 18 U.S. Army Rangers dead, and the Administration quickly abandoned "assertive multilateralism" and nation building in favor of a phased withdrawal of American forces. Later in October the Governor's Island accord on Haiti collapsed when a U.S. cargo ship carrying peacekeepers, the *Harlan County*, turned back rather than face a bunch of thugs on a Haitian dock. Meanwhile, the Administration negotiated inconclusively with North Korea after it refused inspections by the International Atomic Energy Agency (IAEA) and announced its withdrawal from the 1968 Nuclear Nonproliferation Treaty (NPT); Clinton pointed publicly to the extreme seriousness of the North's possession of nuclear weapons but repeatedly watered down his negotiating posture and temporized when Pyongyang failed to respond. Then in May 1994, in the face of Beijing's intransigeance on human rights, Clinton had to abandon publicly his policy on MFN treatment for China and admit that commerce, not morality, was really his top priority.

By this time, the Clinton style of foreign policy had become known in the State Department as "the lurch." It followed naturally from a President inattentive to foreign policy who was surrounded by idealist advisers and pressured by an idealist party in Congress. It was easy, after all, to declare ambitious goals in foreign policy when morality seemed to demand them: *of course* it was the right thing to do to end the bloodshed in Bosnia, build a functioning state in Somalia, restore the elected government in Haiti, or ensure human rights for the Chinese people. Advisers came with the policy papers, and an unwitting President, his experience thin and his attention elsewhere, approved. Only later did it become clear that money was not available, that important members of Congress were not on board, that allies would not cooperate, that it was extremely difficult and far more costly than expected to affect the development of other societies and cultures (indeed, that military force might be needed to do so), that public opinion did not think the goal worth the cost—in short, that the means really necessary to the declared objectives were not at hand. So, either the Administration would reverse itself, as it did on China and Bosnia, or events would humiliate it, as they did in Somalia and Haiti.

In a remarkable interview after he left office, Secretary Christopher admitted a lot of mistakes during the Administration's early years. "We probably allowed the [Somali] mission to get out of hand," he said. "There was mission creep that we didn't want. We should have paid closer attention." In Haiti, the United States had allowed itself to look impotent; it was wrong, Christopher acknowledged, to send a lone warship into Port-au-Prince harbor "without a substantial backup force." On Bosnia, "we should have taken more time to determine a strategy that would have been fully successful." Overall, Christopher candidly concluded, "I wish we had realized earlier how essential U.S. leadership is. That is something we had to learn, or have brought home to us, very forcefully."

Toward an Active Pragmatism

By the winter of 1994–95, however, things seemed to change. First, the Republican victory in the 1994 elections ended any hope of major Clinton domestic initiatives and with it the need to be careful overseas. After all, if the Administration was unable to enact programs like health-care reform when the Democrats controlled Congress, how could it expect to do so now that the Republicans had captured both houses? Second, Clinton learned that foreign affairs need not be simply a political negative, stealing resources from domestic reform and holding the seeds of disastrous entrapment, but that success in statecraft could be a political plus. He also learned a lesson of more doubtful validity: that applying military power to foreign policy goals might not be so dangerous and costly as he had supposed.

Both lessons were learned partly by accident. In late 1994 the Administration was essentially forced by the failure of diplomacy, the draconian effects of economic sanctions on the people of Haiti, and its own rhetoric about democracy to all but invade Haiti in order to redeem its pledges. The threat of force worked, and the President found not only that success without Congress was more possible in foreign than in domestic policy, but also that success abroad could add to perceptions of his power and hence to his political capital for use in the domestic arena. The next summer he had a similar experience with Bosnia. With the war escalating dangerously, Clinton either had to take major risks for peace or be forced to redeem his own commitment of 20,000 U.S. troops to help NATO pull allied forces out of the evolving chaos. This time he actually had to use air power, but the result was the Dayton peace accord ending the Bosnian war and an image of a President who could get things done.

More focused on foreign policy and with such experiences under his belt, Clinton emerged by his fourth year in office as a Democratic pragmatist both more able to limit his Administration's goals to the achievable and more willing to deploy the means, including force, necessary to his ends. He came to understand, as presidential adviser George Stephanopoulos put it, that there was "no real substitute for hand-to-hand personal diplomacy." Clinton was helped by the fact that, although the Democratic caucus on the Hill was arguably more liberal after the 1994 Republican victory than before, it now had fewer votes and thus less power over the White House. In confirmation of

MCCD Libraries

MCC B.J. Harrison Library
Marshalltown, Iowa 50158

27

this pragmatic yet more activist trend, he used the occasion of his own 1996 reelection to rid himself of some of his more idealist advisers. Christopher, Lake and others at lower levels left the Administration, while those who remained seemed chastened by their experiences. Albright, for example, abandoned "assertive multilateralism" for the "doability doctrine": the idea that the United States should only help other countries where it could make a difference at reasonable cost.

Working under that rubric, the Administration applied itself to mediating peace in the Middle East and Northern Ireland, with partial if not complete success. The United States watched but did not intervene when civil war broke out in Zaire. It was cautious about apprehending war criminals in Bosnia when such idealist action might have jeopardized the peace it had helped negotiate, and it opposed the creation of an international criminal court lest Americans find themselves unwitting subjects of its jurisdiction. It also refused to sign an international treaty banning antipersonnel land mines out of concern for the U.S. defensive positions in Korea, and it took a cautious stance when massive human-rights abuses obstructed the birth of nationhood in East Timor, sending only rhetorical condemnation and modest support for international peacekeepers led by others. Similarly, when the UN peacekeeping mission in Sierra Leone fell apart, the Administration quickly made clear that the dispatch of American combat troops was not an option. As the President said in March 1995, "we cannot become involved in every problem we really care about."

Although it was triggered by an idealist response to a massacre of Kosovar civilians at Racak, America's spring 1999 involvement in Kosovo was consistent with the pragmatic posture the Administration had adopted by its second term. In fact, the war demonstrated again that Democratic pragmatism is not a rejection of the party's mission but an idealism restrained by the costs and risks it poses to domestic programs and by the need to be effective in action. At home, the war played out against the background of partisan bitterness and legislative deadlock engendered during the 1998–99 impeachment and trial of the

President, which lowered still further the apparent domestic opportunity costs of risky foreign activism. Internationally, the war not only reflected the Administration's facile view, developed in Haiti and Bosnia, that force could be used at low cost and risk; its prosecution was also restrained (idealists and unilateralists thought too much so) by Clinton's recognition of the need to keep NATO allies on board, a precondition for success via coercive diplomacy rather than outright military conquest.

It is also likely, however, that the Administration did not consider Kosovo as idealist an enterprise as did its critics. Like the Haiti and Dayton interventions described earlier in this chapter, the decision to use military force was to some extent driven by an impulse to redeem earlier policies, as well as to protect already sunk costs, since a failure to end ethnic cleansing in Kosovo might well have jeopardized the U.S. position in Bosnia. More important, however, the Administration saw hard national security interests involved in the prospect of a wider European war and the failure of NATO to deal with its first post-cold-war crisis. Interestingly, in doing so it was following

Reprinted with special permission of - King Features Syndicate

29

the view of American interests set forth by a Republican President, George Bush, who was the first to threaten military action against Serbia if it began ethnic cleansing in Kosovo.

While visiting American troops in Kosovo in June 1999, Clinton told them that wherever in the world "somebody comes after innocent civilians and tries to kill them en masse because of their race, their ethnic background or their religion, and it's within our power to stop it, we will stop it." Many commentators have found in these remarks a new, idealist Clinton doctrine justifying intervention to relieve human suffering worldwide. But the President's more considered post-Kosovo policy was better summed up in his speech to the UN General Assembly in the fall of 1999, when he said not only that "promising too much can be as cruel as caring too little," but that "the way the international community responds [to humanitarian disasters] will depend upon the capacity of countries to act, and on their perceptions of their national interests." It was an apt description of the blend of restraint and idealism that characterizes Democratic pragmatism.

The Battle Over Free Trade

The extent to which the United States should stand against human suffering overseas was not the only foreign policy issue that divided Democrats into pragmatic and idealist factions. Another had to do with the economic pillar of Clinton's statecraft, where the President consistently campaigned and governed as a believer in the benefits of economic globalization and free trade. That position cut across the Democrats' support from blue-collar workers and organized labor, who feared loss of jobs to low-wage countries overseas, and from environmentalists, who considered developing countries' lax pollution controls part of their unfair competitive advantage. Action to protect jobs, working conditions and the environment was, of course, very much in the Democratic tradition of using government to redress inequities and uplift the downtrodden. But idealists tend to be more passionately committed to these causes and to their application overseas as well as at home, whereas

30

Copyright 1997. Distributed by the Los Angeles Times Syndicate. Reprinted with permission.

pragmatists focus more on the overall benefits freer trade promises across American society in economic efficiency, higher-wage job growth and lower consumer prices.

Trade liberalization divided Republicans too, though in their case the line did not run down the center of the party but rather split off only extreme, populist conservatives like Pat Buchanan and Ross Perot, who considered globalization a threat to American sovereignty. Most Republicans supported freer trade as beneficial to U.S. businesses and in line with their laissez-faire approach to the government's role—or preferred lack of it—in the economy. It was not surprising, then, that the Administration got the North American Free Trade Agreement (Nafta) implementing legislation through a Democratic-controlled Congress in 1993 via a Republican majority. The toughest fight was in the House, where then Majority Leader Richard Gephardt (D-Mo.) and Majority Whip David Bonior (D-Mich.) actively worked *against* the legislation, while the President worked *with* Republican Minority Leader Robert Michel (Ill.) and his whip, Newt Gingrich. House Republicans voted for Nafta 132–43, but Democrats voted against it 102-156. Although the Administration later got approval for the Uruguay Round Agreement of the General Agreement on Tariffs and Trade (GATT) creating the World Trade Organization (WTO) by a wider and less divisive margin, it did so only by calling Congress back for a lame-duck session before the Republican majority elected in 1994 took their seats.

Fast-Track Puzzlement

Despite the importance of Republican votes for Nafta and the Uruguay Round, however, Clinton's trade initiatives ran into more rather than less trouble after the Republicans took control of Congress in 1995. The reasons for this puzzling outcome are still a matter of debate. The big remaining issue in 1997–98 was so-called fast-track legislation, giving the President the authority to negotiate trade deals that Congress could only accept or reject but not amend, and the problem was in the House. First, many of the Republican Class of 1994 were probably less likely to vote for freer trade than the Democrats they replaced, because defeated Democrats were either pragmatists who supported free trade or individuals who would not have gone against their President's leadership on this issue, and because some of the new Republicans were populist anti-trade conservatives of the Buchanan stripe. Moreover, delegation of this important issue to the President, always an affront to congressional prerogatives, became all the more offensive to Republicans on the Hill now that it would be from a Republican-controlled Congress to a Democratic President. Second, most observers concluded that Clinton did not lead as strongly on fast track as in the earlier trade fights, perhaps because of his concern over the danger pro-trade votes demonstrably posed for his party. Third, the abstract nature of fast track itself had opposite and perverse effects on the coalitions for and against it: business support for fast track was weaker than for Nafta or WTO because there was no concrete trade treaty with specific benefits at issue, while for antitrade Democrats granting open-ended authority meant turning over movement toward free trade to a Republican Congress and a pro-trade president.

Whatever the complex of reasons, two attempts to get fast-track authority from the 105th Congress ended in failure. Votes in the Senate and House showed strong Republican majorities for fast track and strong Democratic majorities against it, thus confirming a partisan explanation of positions on foreign economic policy (that Republicans would be for free trade and Democrats, in spite of contrary presidential leadership, opposed). But careful inspection reveals a factional, extremes-against-the-middle kind of line-up within the broader partisan one. Republican internationalists were overwhelmingly for fast track as were Democratic pragmatists (at least in the Senate), while Democratic idealists were overwhelmingly against it, along with the most conservative Republican unilateralists.

The final big trade vote of the Clinton Administration—House approval of permanent normal trade relations (PNTR) with China on May 24, 2000—followed similar lines. The overall vote (237–197) was very close to Nafta's (234–200), but the party division was even more pronounced, with about a quarter more Republicans (and a quarter *fewer* Democrats) voting for PNTR than for Nafta. Among Republicans, virtually all of the no votes came from unilateralists, while among Democrats intense lobbying by the President was able to persuade about half the pragmatists but only a third of the idealists followed in this study. The erosion of already weak Democratic support for freer trade, registered at a time when the economy is so much stronger than when the Nafta vote took place in 1993, is eloquent testimony to the fear of economic openness and globalization in many segments of American society. But it also has to do with the greater strategic significance and emotional baggage of China as compared to Mexico (see Chapter 3). Unilateralists like Dana Rohrabacher (R-Calif.), worried about how freer trade might build up China's military capacity, made common cause in the House debate with idealists like Nancy Pelosi (D-Calif.), who railed against Chinese human-rights abuses. In this instance, then, nontrade issues had the effect of heightening the factional splits that already existed on economic grounds. Still, Clinton was able to consolidate his biggest legislative foreign policy victory since Nafta when the Senate voted for PNTR 83–15.

The conclusion that can be drawn from these cases is that trade liberalization splits both parties and pits their pro-trade centrist factions against their antitrade political extremes. Republicans and senators are more likely to be free traders, while Democrats and House members are more likely to be against free trade, but within those parameters the antitrade forces pull most strongly on idealists and (to a lesser extent) unilateralists, while pro-trade forces pull most strongly on internationalists and (somewhat less) on pragmatists. Clearly, new Democratic pragmatists like Clinton have not yet managed to convince the majority of their party on this issue, both because the Democrats' mission heightens their concern about the losers in globalization and because congressional Democrats' political and financial backing comes so heavily from organized labor. The trade issue, more directly connected to domestic economic concerns than virtually any other foreign policy matter, is thus far more divisive and consequential for Democrats than Republicans. Some have argued that the Nafta vote and presidential support for the Uruguay Round resulted in tepid union support for Democrats in the 1994 mid-term election and contributed to the Republican takeover of Congress. In the 2000 campaign, however, the level of union financial and political support for the Democratic ticket seems to indicate that labor has learned its lesson.

3

The Republicans: Unilateralists versus Internationalists

DIVISIONS OVER FOREIGN POLICY among Republicans are, if anything, even more profound and consequential than those of the Democrats. During the cold war the Republican party profited from its hard-line stance against the U.S.S.R.'s Evil Empire; in spite of considerable differences in approach to the problem of Soviet power, Republican Presidents from Eisenhower to Nixon to Reagan and Bush were rarely accused of being soft on communism. But with the cold war over, the Republicans were left without an enemy in the competition for power and wealth that their mission envisioned as the normal order of international affairs. Instead, they were faced with many smaller threats (like crime, drugs and global pollution) rather than other nation-states; a U.S. economy increasingly integrated with and vulnerable to the world economy; an information revolution that brought pictures of humanitarian crises and ethnic conflicts into American living rooms; and a new world order in which businesses, governments and nonstate organizations increasingly cooperated across international boundaries.

The Bush Administration was midwife for the birth of the post-cold-war world and had masterfully fought against old-fashioned aggression by an upstart evil empire in the Persian Gulf. But President Bush had precious little time to define the Republican response to the new world he had helped deliver before being swept from office by Clinton. Instead, just as all the old foreign policy verities were changing, Republicans were forced to watch from their minority status on Capitol Hill as Bush's tactical mastery was replaced by the lurching, inexperienced amateurism of a President who seemed to be trying hard to ignore foreign policy altogether.

No doubt, as he gained his foreign policy sea legs, Clinton would have preferred that his opposition come from the Republican internationalists he had just defeated, but in the 1994 midterm elections the party on the Hill decided to put its fate in the hands of a visionary conservative from Georgia, Newt Gingrich. Gingrich's plan was to run congressional candidates on a nationwide platform, the Contract with America, which would spell out what the Republican party would do if it could gain control of the House of Representatives. The contract was mainly a conservative tract on domestic policy, but it also weighed in against the Administration's assertive multilateralism and perceived antimilitary bias, promising to cut U.S. support for peacekeeping, ensure that U.S. troops would never serve under foreign command, protect the military budget, and build a national missile defense system.

When the Republicans won overwhelmingly, taking control of the House for the first time in 40 years, they could thus point to a foreign policy mandate that not only ran contrary to the Clinton Administration's developing statecraft but was also at considerable variance with that of the Bush Administration. The struggle over foreign policy between the Congress and the White House has thus not only been a struggle between Clinton and Republicans generally, but more especially one between Clinton and the unilateralist faction of Republicans that from 1995 on controlled Congress. What follows is an issue-by-issue examination of this struggle, further illuminating the unilateralist approach to statecraft as well as the Clinton Democratic pragmatist approach (see chart on page 73).

Cutting Resources: Aid and Agency Reorganization

Since 1995 Republican unilateralists in both houses of Congress have demanded and enacted deep cutbacks in all the government agencies conducting U.S. foreign policy. Their most dramatic attack on American diplomatic capabilities was the effort championed by Helms, chairman of the Senate Foreign Relations Committee, to restructure the foreign affairs agencies of the U.S. government, abolishing three of them in the process. In mid-March 1995, Helms unveiled his plan for "a fundamental and revolutionary reinvention of America's foreign policy institutions." He wanted to merge the Agency for International Development (AID), the United States Information Agency (USIA) and the Arms Control and Disarmament Agency (ACDA) into the State Department, in the process terminating half of AID's 3,100 employees while cutting State's staff 14 percent over a three-year period. Together with drastic cuts in U.S. foreign aid, the whole scheme was to save $3.5 billion over five years.

Helms's proposal was the opening gun in what proved to be a three-year struggle. At first the abolition of AID, USIA and ACDA moved rapidly through Congress on party-line votes as part of State Department authorizing legislation; it was even endorsed by Republican internationalists like former Secretaries of State George Shultz, James Baker, and Lawrence Eagleburger. In late May 1995, Clinton was sufficiently alarmed that he called this and other unilateralist legislation "the most isolationist proposals to come before Congress in the last 50 years," while Christopher decried "an extraordinary assault on this and every future President's constitutional authority to manage foreign policy." In June 1995 Democrats filibustered against the legislation in the Senate, and Helms retaliated by holding up

18 ambassadorial nominees, Start II and the Chemical Weapons Convention (CWC). That deadlock persisted until December, when Helms and Senator John Kerry (D-Mass.), negotiating for Clinton, reached agreement on a compromise plan. But unilateralists so altered the compromise on its way through the House that Clinton vetoed it in April 1996.

"MEXICO CITY" LANGUAGE

ADOPTED BY EXECUTIVE ORDER in the Reagan and Bush Administrations with the effect of essentially ending U.S. support for family-planning overseas, the so-called Mexico City policy was repealed the same way by Clinton shortly after he took office. From 1995 on, Representative Smith tried to restore it by repeatedly attaching language to appropriation and authorization bills for the State Department and foreign aid that would have prohibited U.S. support to family-planning organizations overseas if they performed or lobbied for abortions, even if they used their own money. The Senate, for its part, repeatedly refused such language, but GOP leaders in the House backed their conservative members on it, leading to long delays in congressional action. When bills including the language did eventually go forward, Clinton invariably vetoed them. In 1996, 1997 and 1998, Mexico City language was ultimately dropped in order to get the President's signature on appropriations bills, but in the process conservatives managed to restrict assistance for international family planning to $385 million a year (down from an earlier high of over half a billion) disbursed on a strict 8 percent a month basis. Each year, though, the result of the prolonged stalemate was to kick appropriations (along with some authorization language) into last-minute omnibus packages. In these Clinton usually got more of his program than in the earlier, individual bills, partly because Republicans feared being blamed for another government shutdown like the one in late 1995. The tactic certainly caused enormous disorder, delay, and confusion in the legislative process; whether it benefited the unilateralist or conservative cause overall is much harder to prove.

By the time foreign affairs agency reorganization resurfaced in the 105th Congress, Clinton and the Republicans had been reconfirmed in their jobs by the voters and a new secretary of state, Madeleine Albright, had provided assurances to Helms on the issue at her confirmation hearings. Accordingly, on April 17, 1997—the same day that Helms cleared the CWC for the floor—Clinton signed off on a reorganization plan that went further in some ways than the one he'd vetoed the previous year. It merged ACDA and USIA into State, along with some of AID's administrative structure, but it did so without significant personnel downsizing or budgetary savings. Although legislation passed by the Senate in June was tougher on AID than Clinton's plan, the real problem arose in the House, where Representative Christopher Smith (R-N.J.) attached so-called Mexico City language, prohibiting the United States from supporting family-planning organizations overseas (see box). Though more a conservative domestic issue than a unilateralist foreign policy one, this prohibition was totally unacceptable to Democrats and even to moderate Republicans in the Senate, so the refusal of House social conservatives to give it up left the Congress unable to pass any authorization bill at all for the rest of the year.

Foreign affairs reorganization therefore stalled until 1998, when Speaker Gingrich thought he saw a way to use it, Clinton's desire for UN and International Monetary Fund (IMF) funding, and the Mexico City language issue to forge Republican unity and embarrass the Democrats in an election year. Gingrich incorporated all three elements into HR 1757, the "Foreign Affairs Reform and Restructuring Act of 1998," and the Republican leadership got it past both unilateralists in the House (who opposed UN funding) and Republican moderates in the Senate (who opposed its Mexico City language). Again the President vetoed the legislation because of the international family-planning issue, but the reorganization language from HR 1757 was incorporated into the Omnibus Consolidated and Emergency Supplemental Appropriations Act for FY1999, signed by Clinton on October 21, 1998. ACDA and

USIA were sacrificed and Helms had most of his reorganization, but on terms crafted by the President.

Unilateralist Assaults

The successful unilateralist push to cut the State Department budget and abolish other U.S. foreign policy agencies was done in parallel with an assault on bilateral foreign assistance. To be sure, the Congress had been reducing foreign aid for years before Clinton became President and continued to do so even during his first two years in office, when it was still controlled by the Democrats. But from 1995 on, Republican unilateralists, especially in the House, went after the aid budget with ferocity, targeting support of international financial institutions and aid for poorer nations, particularly in Africa. Except for nuclear-threat-reduction programs, conservatives also repeatedly tried to cut aid to Russia—because of its nuclear cooperation with and missile sales to Iran, because of Moscow's support for Serbia in the Kosovo conflict, because of Russian wars in Chechnya, or because of corruption in Moscow and the paralysis of reform there. House Majority Leader Richard Armey (R-Tex.) summed it up this way in 1999: "The stated purpose of the Clinton-Gore policy was to help Russia become a peaceful and productive free-market democracy. Instead, Russia has become a looted and bankrupt zone of nuclearized anarchy."

In the end, the Administration was usually able to get most of the aid funding it requested from the Hill by vetoing appropriations bills and forcing Republicans into omnibus spending negotiations like that in which reorganization was accomplished in 1998. In some instances, however, unilateralists were able to assemble and maintain coalitions that effectively blocked foreign aid. That happened on the first foreign policy test Clinton faced with the new Congress, his January 1995 effort to get approval for $40 billion in U.S. loan guarantees to stabilize the Mexican peso after its abrupt devaluation on December 20, 1994. Because it was seen as a Nafta-related trade issue, the peso crisis recreated the unilateralist-idealist coalition that had opposed the earlier trade pact and would later deny Clinton fast-track authority. Unilateralists like Representative Duncan Hunter (R-Calif.), who opposed the rescue outright ("This is a Wall Street bailout, not a Main Street bailout"), joined with idealist Democrats like Minority Whip Bonior, who wanted to attach labor and environmental conditions to the Mexican aid that most Republicans would not accept. Despite strong support from Republicans like Speaker Gingrich, Representative Jim Leach (Iowa) and former President George Bush, the 1994 defeat of many pro-trade pragmatist Democrats—and their replacement with unilateralist Republicans—changed the math of the confrontation from the winning Nafta/Uruguay Round configuration. In the end, Clinton was forced to help Mexico without recourse to Congress by using the Treasury's Exchange Stabilization Fund.

Opposing the IMF and the UN

Unilateralists' opposition to foreign aid went beyond the bilateral U.S. program to include multilateral assistance and American contributions to international financial institutions, especially the IMF. Early in 1997 Clinton requested $3.4 billion for an IMF facility called the New Arrangements to Borrow (NAB) designed to support sagging Third World currencies. Though the Senate foreign operations bill included the amount, House unilateralists insisted on its deletion from the FY1998 foreign aid appropriations bill when they were forced to give up Mexico City language.

In 1998 Clinton upped the ante, again requesting the $3.4 billion for the NAB but adding another $14.5 billion for an IMF quota increase. By now the Asian financial crisis that had begun late in 1997 had become a full-blown economic collapse, spreading to other emerging markets and depressing U.S. exports. The Senate again provided the full amount, internationalist Budget Committee Chairman Pete Domenici (R-N.M.) warning that failure "to approve these funds could cause the American economy to go down." But although the House committee now allowed the $3.4 billion, it denied Clinton's larger

©Tribune Media Services, Inc. All Rights Reserved. Reprinted with permission.

quota request, and the unilateralist attack on IMF funding intensified, led by Armey, Majority Whip Tom DeLay (Tex.), and Jim Saxton (N.J.). "The IMF is an anachronism in today's modern global economy," said DeLay; "We ought to be talking in terms of phasing out the IMF."

The bill was reported out and passed by the full House with only the $3.4 billion for the NAB but with Mexico City language and with IMF reform requirements that unilateralist Senator Jon Kyl (R.-Ariz.) had tried unsuccessfully to attach in the Senate. Clinton was willing to negotiate some IMF reforms, but he argued that debating the operations of the fire department was "no excuse for refusing to supply...[it] with water while the fire is burning." In the end, pressure from farm and business groups persuaded Republicans to accept the full IMF funding with conditions that merely restated reforms the IMF was already undertaking. Clinton got his $17.9 billion in the FY1999 Omnibus Spending bill signed October 21, 1998, the same bill that enacted foreign affairs agencies reorganization.

The issue of IMF funding was especially sensitive for

unilateralists because it combined their opposition to foreign aid with another unilateralist *bête noire*, international organizations. In fact, conservatives' negative views toward all government often produced a strident opposition to international agencies, which are forms of government at the international level that many unilateralists believe threaten American sovereignty. In 1995 Helms recommended "terminating or greatly reducing" funds for a wide variety of UN specialized and affiliated agencies, including the UN Development Program, the UN Fellowship Program, the UN Population Fund, and the International Labor Organization, which he labeled "archaic" and "ill-suited to an era in which the role of labor unions is vastly diminished." He later argued for a 50 percent cut in UN staff and a 75 percent cut in the secretary-general's budget. On the House side, unilateralists were perhaps even more opposed to international bodies of all kinds, and in 1997 a proposal by Ron Paul (R-Tex.) requiring immediate U.S. withdrawal from the UN got votes from DeLay, Hunter, Rohrabacher, Joe Scarborough (R-Fla.), Tom Coburn (R-Okla.), Steve Largent (R-Okla.) and Rules Committee Chairman Gerald H.B. Solomon (R-N.Y.).

The most serious and prolonged unilateralist attack on international organizations involved denying over a billion dollars in U.S. arrearages to the UN, money withheld for years in spite of treaty obligations the United States had freely and constitutionally assumed under the UN Charter. The UN put the amount owed at $1.52 billion in annual dues and assessments for peacekeeping operations, but unilateralists argued that it was really much lower and sparred with the Administration for years over how much the United States should pay and whether the payment should be tied to further UN reforms. Finally, following Helms's 1997 agreement with Clinton on foreign affairs agency consolidation, he and Senator Joseph Biden (D-Del.) negotiated a deal providing $819 million in arrearages while forgiving the UN $107 million in debt to the United States, provided the organization accepted the settlement as payment in full and also agreed to a permanent 20 percent reduction in the share of the UN budget paid by the United States. (As many as two dozen other conditions were also included in the Helms-Biden deal, including adoption of a negative growth UN budget and the right of the U.S. General Accounting Office (GAO) to audit UN programs.) When internationalist Senator Richard Lugar (Ind.) proposed that the arrearages be paid more quickly and unconditionally, his amendment was solidly voted against by unilateralists and, though supported by most Democratic pragmatists, was unable to garner enough Republican internationalist and Democratic idealist support to pass.

The Helms-Biden deal was enacted by the Senate in 1997, 1998 and 1999, but each year House conservatives attached the Mexico City language to it, ensuring either deadlock in the Congress or a presidential veto. Finally, amid another set of furious, last-minute budget negotiations during the first two weeks in November 1999, the President got his UN arrearages—plus $2.6 billion more in foreign aid and a two-year State Department authorization. He did, however, accept that the Mexico City language would for the first time become law, albeit in an appropriations measure that would expire at the end of the fiscal year and in a form that included the authority to waive it altogether at the cost of only 3 percent of the appropriated family-planning funds. Clinton yielded partly because of the other elements of the package, partly because the United States was at last facing the loss of its vote in the General Assembly if it did not pay at least $350 million in back dues by the end of the year, and partly because the authority to call the back dues "emergency spending" (and thereby exempt them from the 1997 budget caps) would soon expire. Most important of all, as Senator Tom Daschle (D-S.D.) saw it, Clinton yielded because "we simply cannot tell the world that we're going to shrink from our responsibilities at the UN" over a domestic dispute on abortion.

The Military and Peacekeeping

Although unilateralists have tried to reduce or abolish funding for cooperative tools of statecraft like foreign aid, international organizations, information and exchange programs and traditional diplomacy, they want to expand it for the ultimate unilateral instrument of policy: the military. The Contract with America argued for the "restoration of the essential parts of our national security funding to strengthen our national defenses and maintain our credibility around the world," and unilateralists have led the broader Republican party in repeatedly criticizing Clinton for allowing a return to the hollow army of the post-Vietnam years. Quite plausibly, they contended that the Administration's actions in Haiti, Iraq and the former Yugoslavia increased the operations tempo of American forces, but that the Administration failed to provide the additional resources needed to sustain them. "What we are witnessing," warned Representative Floyd Spence (R-S.C.) during the Kosovo war, "is the debilitating cost of and increased geopolitical risks associated with an undersized, under-funded, and overextended U.S. military...." Joined by many Democratic pragmatists, unilateralists not only voted additional billions for the military but also successfully pushed the Administration to increase its own defense requests. The budget comparison table on page 46 therefore understates the difference between Clinton and the Republicans on spending for national defense, but it clearly shows the unilateralist reluctance to fund the State Department, foreign aid, and other cooperative tools of statecraft in the international affairs account.

Interestingly, however, unilateralists' support for a strong American military does not automatically translate into support for military alliances. Although the Contract with America urged NATO's rapid expansion into Eastern Europe, unilateralists' attitudes toward NATO varied. Most unilateralists were still worried about the Russian threat and saw NATO as an important facet of American military power, and they were supportive of the alliance despite its being an international organization. But a few who discounted the Russian threat or viewed NATO more as an international organization than an adjunct to the U.S. military argued that it was a vestige of the cold war that should now be abolished. When the Senate overwhelmingly approved the first round of NATO expansion on

DEFENSE AND INTERNATIONAL AFFAIRS BUDGETS

National Defense
(in billions of dollars)

FISCAL YEAR	CLINTON REQUEST	CONGRESS BUDGET	% DIFFERENCE	ACTUAL APPROP.
1996	258.3	265.4	3%	265.0
1997	255.0	266.4	4%	266.2
1998	266.0	269.0	1%	272.4
1999	271.6	none		288.1
2000	281.6	290.0	3%	294.1
2001	306.3	310.8	1%	

International Affairs
(in billions of dollars)

FISCAL YEAR	CLINTON REQUEST	CONGRESS BUDGET	% DIFFERENCE	ACTUAL APPROP.
1996	21.2	18.3	-14%	18.1
1997	19.4	18.2	-6%	18.2
1998	23.0	19.0	-17%	19.0
1999	20.2	none		23.6
2000	21.3	17.7	-17%	23.9
2001	22.8	20.0	-12%	

Source: Terry L. Deibel

April 30, 1998, the few no votes came mainly from internationalists and idealists: from the Left of *each* party.

Moreover, unilateralists' eagerness to *fund* military power should not be confused with a readiness to *use* it, except to deter or respond to attacks on the United States. Perhaps their least favorite use of American forces is for peacekeeping, a UN-sponsored approach to messy Third World problems that furthers idealist causes in which unilateralists do not believe, turns the military into a cooperative instrument at some cost to its war-fighting capabilities, and offends nationalism by placing U.S. troops under the aegis of international organizations.

One antipeacekeeping tack taken by Republicans was to try to prohibit placing U.S. troops under foreign command, a cause that seemed all the more urgent due to the widespread (though erroneous) belief that botched UN-command arrangements had contributed to the tragic deaths of American servicemen in Somalia. "Nameless UN commanders, committed to questionable military tactics driven by a UN bureaucracy with no public accountability should not decide" what happens to American soldiers, wrote Senator Mitch McConnell (R-Ky.); "Not in Somalia, not in Bosnia, not in Haiti."

Another approach was to limit U.S. funding of all UN peacekeeping, with or without U.S. troops. UN Ambassador Richard Holbrooke thought that peacekeeping funds were a "terrific bargain" because they allowed the United States a say in such operations without paying the whole cost or in many cases even putting U.S. troops in harm's way. But Representative Rohrabacher found a "message" in the 1994 election that "Americans have sacrificed their lives and well-being for an ungrateful world for far too long.... We don't want to be the patsy of the world any more." Republican unilateralists advocated deducting the amount the Defense Department spent for operations in support of peacekeeping from UN assessments for them. Since the former exceeded the latter, unilateralists like Burton and Representative J.C. Watts (R-Okla.) argued that the UN actually owed the United States money. Such calculations would have effectively wiped out direct U.S. financial support of peacekeeping and threatened (as Secretary Christopher argued) "to end UN peacekeeping overnight." That outcome, Clinton warned, "would place U.S. forces at greater risk by forcing us to act unilaterally or not at all."

In fact, acting not at all was exactly what the unilateralists had in mind when it came to most of the Clinton overseas interventions. They simply did not believe U.S. national interests in places like Somalia, Haiti, Bosnia or Kosovo justified spending American money or risking American lives. But Republican unilateralists found that opposing peacekeeping was a frustrating enterprise because cutting money for peacekeeping often meant cutting money for the Pentagon. If the Congress refused to appropriate funds to reimburse the military for its peacekeeping expenses, the money would simply come out of other training and equipment accounts, contributing to the "hollowing out" of the military which Republicans so opposed. Opposition to particular peacekeeping enterprises in which the United States was involved was even trickier, for it could be equated with not supporting American troops in action abroad.

Dilemmas of Inaction

These dilemmas can be seen in congressional action on Bosnia and Kosovo. Two days before the Dayton peace conference began, the House undercut U.S. diplomacy by passing a resolution warning the President not to deploy U.S. peacekeepers in Bosnia without Congress's consent. Then, the day before the Dayton accords were formally signed in Paris, freshmen Republicans nearly destroyed them by bringing the House to within eight votes of cutting off funds for American peacekeepers' deployment, already under way; the Republican Class of 1994 voted in favor of the cutoff 64–8. Suspicion of the Dayton enterprise was strong in both parties, and while arguments that the United States must lead in Europe were persuasive to internationalist Gingrich, his colleague from Georgia, John Linder, typified the unilateralist attitude by saying that he was "not the least bit interested in the prestige of NATO." Once U.S. peacekeepers were in place, unilateralists (and some idealists) repeatedly attempted to cut off their funding, partly in response to the Administration's fudging of the forces' withdrawal deadlines, but also because they simply opposed U.S. involvement.

A similar pattern was evident three-and-a-half years later over Kosovo, although this time what began as opposition to peacekeeping ended as opposition to war. By voting against U.S. participation in a postsettlement peacekeeping force for Kosovo, unilateralists in the House weakened the Administration's efforts to force Slobodan Milosevic to accept a peace agreement negotiated at Rambouillet, France, and unilateralists in both houses opposed resolutions authorizing air operations against Yugoslavia. In fact, Republicans divided along clear unilateralist-internationalist lines over support of the conflict and how deeply the United States should commit to victory. DeLay repeatedly called it Clinton's war and urged his colleagues not to "take ownership" of it, while Lott praised Representative Curt Weldon's (R-Pa.) Vienna, Austria, mission to promulgate an unconditional peace plan with members of the Russian Duma, and urged Americans to "give peace a chance here." But internationalists like Senator John Warner (R-Va.) argued that it was not Clinton's war but America's, and that the stakes were very high: "It's not just the credibility of NATO; it's the credibility of the United States...." These Republicans began urging the President to do more to win. Senator Lugar thought that Milosevic's capitulation would require at least a threat to go beyond air power—"The diplomacy won't start until our President stops saying 'no' to ground troops"— and Senator John McCain (R-Ariz.) began pushing for the soldiers' immediate use, arguing that "we are in it, now we must win it." Unilateralists, however, led the House to pass a resolution on party lines that blocked the President from using ground forces without its approval.

Meanwhile Republicans struggled to use the power of the purse as leverage *against* the war while at the same time *using* the war to fund military requirements they thought Clinton had long neglected. House appropriations chairman C.W. Bill Young (Fla.) thought Congress should make up not only the direct costs of the fighting but indirect costs to the military's capabilities—"we are wearing out troops and wearing out equipment"—and Republicans gladly doubled Clinton's wartime supplemental request to force an increase in defense spending across the board. When, in spite of everything, Milosevic finally capitulated, unilateralists' frustration came to a head. Unable to credit Clinton with success, they called it a "humanitarian disaster," "a settlement we could probably have had at the start," and "a relief, not a victory."

Opposing Cooperative Diplomacy

In addition to opposing the Administration's involvement in UN peacekeeping and what they considered misguided idealist interventions, unilateralists often have used their power of the purse to obstruct American diplomatic efforts. For example, after the President's successful mediation between Israel and the Palestinians at the Wye River Conference Center in Maryland in October 1998, they refused for more than a year to fund his $1.8 billion aid commitment to Israel and the Palestinian Authority. Unilateralists have also repeatedly withheld U.S. aid for Haiti following the 1994 U.S. intervention. While the Administration deliberately denied committing itself to nation building there after the debacle in Somalia, Republicans distrusted President Jean-Bertrand Aristide and wanted to show that Haiti's endemic political violence vitiated any claim by Clinton that his "restoration" of democratic rule had been a success.

Confront Rather than Cooperate

Given their competitive mission, Republicans have been particularly upset with Administration efforts to deal diplomatically with countries that are obvious competitors or even apparent enemies of the United States, like North Korea, China or Iraq. Their charge was that Clinton was insufficiently vigilant against potential threats to American security, and the underlying assumption seemed to be that confrontation rather than cooperative statecraft is the way to deal with states that oppose American power. Again, the tactic adopted to obstruct the Clinton policy was simply to deny the funding necessary to follow through on cooperative agreements.

A case in point was the U.S.-North Korean Agreed Framework, laboriously negotiated after the North Koreans stymied the IAEA inspection regime in their country and threatened to withdraw from the NPT. Finally concluded in October 1994 after several false starts, the Agreed Framework provided that the North Koreans would dismantle their nuclear-weapons program in return for two 1,000-megawatt light-water nuclear-power reactors, provision of heating oil and progressive normalization of diplomatic and trade relations with the United States.

The deal was anything but a clean end to the nuclear threat from North Korea, and the North continued to take actions that seemed to cast its good faith in doubt and highlighted the potential threat posed to the West. While the Clinton Administration argued that the Agreed Framework was nevertheless the best of a variety of unsatisfying options and far better than ineffective sanctions or a horrific war, Republican unilateralists countered that the Administration was doing nothing to head off what it had itself called the most serious of all post-cold-war threats to the United States. So the unilateralists began a multiyear effort to require various sorts of North Korean good behavior in return for U.S. money, conditions that, while apparently reasonable in themselves, would certainly have sabotaged the deal. Most years the Administration succeeded in getting the aid money it had promised North Korea without crippling restrictions by using its veto and relying on end-of-the-year omnibus spending negotiations, but the Republican unilateralist position was hardly in doubt.

Another putative U.S. enemy that has loomed large in Republican concerns is China. After abandoning its failed effort to correct China's abusive human-rights practices in 1994, the Clinton Administration pursued a policy of "strategic engagement," based on the historic gamble that steadily opening trade and active diplomatic and military relations with the world's last Communist giant would eventually lead to its political liberalization. Given their laissez-faire economic predilections and business connections, Republicans were not likely to object to a policy based on freer trade; in fact, the annual June renewals of China's MFN status passed Congress on Republican votes. But given their competitive view of the world, Republicans in general (and unilateralists in particular) were also deeply concerned about the growing power that economic growth was giving China and fearful that its steady military buildup would eventually bring it into conflict with the United States. Representative Doug Bereuter (R-Nebr.) admitted that "a significant amount of support exists in the Congress, especially in my party and especially in the House," for the idea that China was the new enemy, and aides to several unilateralist legislators formed a so-called Blue Team to publicize and energize an American reaction to the growing threat.

Adrian Raeside

As in the North Korea case, Republicans, and especially unilateralists in Congress, repeatedly pushed anti-China legislation that, while reasonable on its merits, would have had the effect of destroying the Administration's efforts at engagement. China's repressive Communist government was one few congressmen of any party wanted to be caught defending, so it was easy for Republicans to find allies on anti-China legislation. Democratic idealists (who abhorred Beijing's human-rights practices and opposed free trade) made common cause with socially conservative Republicans (who condemned China's repression of Christians and compulsory abortions). A good example of what could result was a five-day orgy of anti-China legislating in late 1997, just after the Clinton summit with Chinese President Jiang Zemin, when the House overwhelmingly passed no fewer than nine bills to, among other things, fund human-rights monitors at American diplomatic posts in China, oppose international loans to Beijing, provide more funds for

Radio Free Asia, ban companies dealing with China's army from America, and deny visas to officials engaging in religious persecution. Though the bills were mainly symbolic and died in the Senate, pragmatist Representative Hamilton found himself virtually alone in arguing that it did not serve "American interests today to paint China...as a second evil empire."

To unilateralists it seemed obvious not only that China was the new threat but that Clinton's engagement policy was not preventing Beijing from, for example, selling missiles and nuclear weapons to rogue states or threatening Taiwan. Administration policy toward China was therefore an even richer target of attack than China itself. Helms charged the Administration with "kowtowing to the Chinese Communists" and of following a policy of outright "appeasement," while Representative Christopher Cox (R-Calif.) said that Clinton had given China's leaders "the full Lewinsky." Such attacks took on an even uglier aspect when, in mid-1998, Representative Armey contended that a contractor who had contributed large amounts of money to the Democratic party had been given "special dispensation" to sell the Chinese technology "that would enable them to effectively target their nuclear weapons to the United States." Cox was appointed chairman of an investigating committee, and, following Clinton's impeachment trial, it charged that China had stolen design secrets from U.S. nuclear-weapons laboratories and that Clinton was covering up the espionage to protect his policy of engagement.

Unilateralists Capitalize on Taiwan

The unilateralists' favorite anti-China target has been Taiwan, an island that has been independent in fact since the Communist Revolution but that Beijing considers a renegade province. Since the United States opened contact with Beijing in the early 1970s, Administrations of both parties have maintained a studied ambiguity regarding Taiwan, arming it for defense against military pressure or invasion by the mainland, but accepting China's insistence that there is but one China and limiting government relations with the island to unofficial channels. Unilateralists have wanted to break that ambiguity, knowing that even a gesture as mild as granting a visa to Taiwan's president for a personal visit to the United States (as the Congress forced the Administration to do in 1995) guaranteed a vitriolic reaction from Beijing. Rather than engage China diplomatically on the issue, they pushed legislation that would require Clinton to recognize Taiwan outright and pledge to defend it against attack. Their most successful effort was the Taiwan Security Enhancement Act, which passed the House 341–70 on February 1, 2000, with all factions in favor except pragmatists. Written by Helms and DeLay, it would strengthen U.S.-Taiwanese military ties and give Congress a bigger voice in U.S. weapons sales to the island. Pragmatist Representative Tom Lantos (D-Calif.) warned that the bill would "stir up a hornet's nest of instability in the region," and Helms happily agreed: "Some are going to say this is provocative. They will claim that doing these things will upset the U.S. relationship with China. This is true. The Red Chinese won't like this bill." Unilateralists also pushed for American missile defenses for Taiwan, a move Beijing characterized as an encroachment on China's sovereignty and territorial integrity.

Another contested situation in which conservative Republicans made clear their preference for unilateral, confrontational statecraft over multilateral, cooperative diplomacy was Iraq. Though it often threatened and used force against Iraq, the Clinton Administration initially dropped the Bush Administration's demand for Iraqi President Saddam Hussein's overthrow and adopted a policy—of containment via sanctions and the UN weapons inspection regime (Unscom)—that depended on consensus within the UN Security Council. Accordingly, when Unscom was challenged by Saddam in early 1998 and the United States found little international support for responding militarily, Clinton endorsed an agreement reached with Baghdad by UN Secretary General Kofi Annan to defuse the crisis. Senate Majority Leader Lott promptly denounced Annan for appeasement, and Senator Helms compared him to British Prime Minister Neville Chamberlain returning from the

Munich conference of 1938, which appeased Hitler's conquests in Europe. Lott also added $38 million to the State Department authorization bill to provide humanitarian and political support for Saddam's opponents, fund a Radio Free Iraq, and sponsor a UN criminal tribunal to indict Iraqi officials.

Although the Administration threatened to use force if Saddam violated his pledge to Annan, it intervened over the summer of 1998 to stop some challenge inspections by Unscom and failed to follow through on its threat when Saddam terminated all contact with the inspection regime in August. Instead, still finding no support internationally for military action, it responded to Iraqi challenges throughout the fall with a stepped-up effort to rebuild a Security Council consensus. Meanwhile, Lott and Representative Benjamin Gilman (R-N.Y.), chairman of the House International Affairs Committee, sponsored legislation expressing the sense of the Congress that Saddam's overthrow should be the policy of the United States and authorizing $97 million in U.S. military aid to opposition groups. In the midst of the crisis in early October 1998, this Iraq Liberation Act passed the House 360–38 and the Senate by voice vote. Although the Administration remained skeptical of the ability of opposition groups to overthrow Saddam, Clinton signed the legislation and adopted a policy of "containment plus regime change," complete with a Special Representative for the Transition in Iraq. By December, when diplomacy had clearly failed to return inspectors to Iraq, Clinton fell back on a program of massive air strikes that predictably drew sharp Russian and French condemnation.

Arms Control and Security

The unilateralists' opposition to Administration policy on North Korea, China/Taiwan and Iraq reflected an underlying view that potential military threats to the United States cannot be adequately dealt with through multilateral and cooperative means. It is not surprising, then, to find that unilateralists were also opposed to most arms-control treaties and regimes. The Chemical Weapons Convention (CWC), which entered into force in 1997, was a particularly interesting case in point, since it was signed by President Bush and is therefore as much a Republican internationalist treaty as a Democratic pragmatist one. Still, Helms and Senator Strom Thurmond (R-S.C.) vowed to block the treaty indefinitely, despite the fact that the United States had decided years earlier to destroy all its own chemical weapons by 2004.

Clinton invested more political capital on the CWC than on any foreign affairs issue since Nafta, and he won a solid 74–26 vote in favor of ratification. The vote was instructive. Both idealist and pragmatist Democrats voted for the treaty and to delete all five killer amendments proposed by Helms. Backed by testimony from Bush's National Security Adviser Brent Scowcroft, Republican internationalists also voted for the treaty, but a few voted to keep one or more of the killer amendments. Unilateralist Republicans, however, mostly voted against the treaty and for the killer amendments, although a few, including Lott and McConnell, found a less obvious way to oppose the treaty by voting for it but also for all the killer amendments.

Clinton's CTBT Defeat

Clinton was less successful with the other centerpiece of his arms-control efforts, the Comprehensive Test Ban Treaty (CTBT). Whereas the CWC was a Bush treaty, it was Clinton who signed the CTBT on September 24, 1996, and at the unilateralists' least favorite venue, UN headquarters in New York City. Helms took no action on the treaty for two years after Clinton submitted it to the Senate, but beginning in the winter of 1998–99 Senator Kyl and a small group of unilateralists began collecting commitments against it from their colleagues, and by early summer they were confident of a blocking third. Meanwhile, the Democrats, all unawares and wanting to get U.S. approval before an October conference on the treaty in Vienna, Austria, began publicly demanding a vote. They kept up the pressure all summer, ultimately threatening to block all Senate business unless the treaty was released.

Suddenly, on the last day of September, Lott offered an up-or-down vote, and the Democrats realized that the treaty would fail. Negotiations with the White House to delay the vote foundered on Lott's demand that Clinton promise not to bring the treaty up again. Although 62 senators (including 24 Republicans) signed a letter urging that action be postponed, legislative efforts to stop the majority leader were considered an assault on the Republican control of the Senate and voted down along strict party lines. Then, on October 13, 1999, the treaty itself went down to defeat 48–51, handing Clinton the biggest foreign policy defeat of his presidency. Internationalist Republicans split on the treaty vote itself, but virtually all of them had signed the letter urging postponement. Unilateralist Republicans, on the other hand, all voted against the treaty, and virtually none signed the postponement letter.

Given unilateralists' opposition to treaty cooperation against the proliferation of weapons of mass destruction (WMD) and to diplomatic restraints on the rogue states (like North Korea or Iraq) that might use them against the United States, one might ask what alternative they proposed. The answer, in addition to a strong American military, was rapid deployment of a national missile defense (NMD) system. NMD was a less elaborate but still extraordinarily ambitious version of Reagan's "Star Wars" program, designed to protect the United States from attack by a small number of ballistic missiles launched by rogue states or terrorists. Though some fiscal conservatives among them worried about the high cost of the program, Republicans tried repeatedly from 1995 to 1998 to enact legislation that would require the United States to deploy an NMD system, and in 1995 and 1996 they raised Clinton's requested appropriations for the project by amounts ranging from 40 percent to over 100 percent. Though he was willing to see research continue, Clinton resisted any commitment to deploy an NMD system, not only because the highly complex weapon was far short of being ready and would deal with only one of the many ways that WMD could be detonated on American soil, but also because U.S. intelligence agencies had determined that the threat it was designed to meet lay at least 15 years in the future.

Most serious of all, deployment ran counter to the 1972 U.S.-Soviet Antiballistic Missile Treaty (ABM), which the President considered the cornerstone of the entire structure of great-power arms control. When Clinton vetoed the first FY1996 defense authorization over the issue he said that the bill would have set U.S. policy "on a collision course with the ABM Treaty" and would thereby "jeopardize continued Russian implementation of the Start I Treaty as well as Russian ratification of the Start II Treaty." Senator Sam Nunn (D-Ga.), who felt compelled to vote against the Pentagon spending measure for the first time in his Senate career because of NMD, considered it "the most gigantic step backwards in arms control that we've taken in years." But the destructive arms-control implications of NMD made it all the more attractive to unilateralists, who distrusted multilateral guarantees and found Senator Byron Dorgan (D-N.D.) naïve or worse when he argued that "arms control is giving us missile defense that works, right now."

Still, the NMD issue did not catch on in the 1996 campaign, and neither that year nor the next could Republicans bring it to a vote in either house of Congress. In 1998, however, nuclear blasts by India and Pakistan, North Korea's testing of a three-stage missile over Japan, and intelligence assessments that Iran might soon have an operational ballistic missile brought Republicans to within a single vote of ending the Democratic filibuster against NMD legislation. Apparently deciding that it was about to lose control of the issue, the Administration announced in late January 1999 that it would spend $6.6 billion over five years to build an NMD system, and in mid-March Clinton accepted legislation committing the United States to deploy it "as soon as technologically possible" in return for a congressional reaffirmation of arms-control negotiations with the Russians. Unilateralists like Representative Weldon and Senator Kyl were delighted but skeptical, for although Defense Secretary William Cohen had said that Washington would deploy the system even if the Russians disapproved, the Administration made it clear in later months that it was determined not to sacrifice relations with Russia or the arms-control treaty structure in the process. As Deputy Secretary of State Strobe Talbott put it, "we've got to find a way of reconciling not just the desirability but the imperative of maintaining the ABM Treaty while at the same time giving not just the United States but other countries as well—including Russia—the capacity to deal with this new threat."

The Internationalist Alternative

The unilateralist approach to American foreign policy as expressed in the issues detailed above embodies a paradoxical reaction to the U.S. position as the sole remaining superpower. On the one hand, unilateralists are confident enough in American superiority that they believe the United States can do whatever needs to be done in the world by itself; otherwise, a unilateralist policy would make no sense. On the other hand, they seem fearful that the country is not powerful enough to protect and advance its interests if it operates within international organizations, multilateral treaty regimes or by means of cooperative bilateral diplomacy. Internationalist Republicans are free of this unilateralist fear. And because they are confident that the United States can adequately define and defend its interests multilaterally as well as unilaterally, cooperatively as well as confrontationally, internationalists are sometimes willing to act in situations where American interests are not so great or the threats to those interests so severe as to justify the cost and risk of unilateral action.

Republican internationalists would, to be sure, avoid involvement in many situations in which Democratic pragmatists (and certainly idealists) might act. They would generally limit armed interventions to situations involving clear national interests in security or prosperity—like the Iraqi invasion of Kuwait, for example, but not like the military's overthrow of democratic rule in Haiti. But as Bush's 1992 intervention in Somalia showed, their response to crises of less compelling interest is not necessarily to do nothing, a stance that opens unilateralists up to charges of isolationism. Where risks appear to be manageable and intervention effective, internationalists are willing to act, leading multilateral coalitions to keep costs commensurate with interests.

More strikingly, even in cases where the nation's vital interests are endangered, Republican internationalists are willing to act in cooperation with other states—even if that means scaling back maximum American demands somewhat—in an effort to get the job done at lower cost and risk. President Bush, after all, not only used the UN to legitimate his actions in the Persian Gulf war; he also accepted restrictions on American war objectives to sustain a coalition that both paid for the war and reduced the diplomatic risk the United States ran in attacking an Arab, Islamic state. As subsequent problems with Saddam's Iraq have shown, how far one should compromise policy objectives in order to act cooperatively is a debatable question. Still, Republican internationalists believe that multilateral organizations and coalitions can be made to serve important national interests via strong American leadership.

Heng/Cartoonists &Writers Syndicate/cartoonweb.com

The center of internationalist power in Washington after the Republicans took control of Congress was a group of about a dozen of the party's senators, including Majority Leader Robert Dole (Kans.) until he began running for President in 1996, when he abandoned many of his own long-standing internationalist positions in an effort to appeal to the party's right-wing base. Internationalist Republicans were also found among more senior Republicans in the House, including Speakers Gingrich and Hastert. But the second tier of House leadership was in unilateralist hands, and the size of the Class of 1994, combined with their biennial electoral need to define themselves in opposition to the President and the slow shrinkage in the overall Republican majority, left House internationalists unwilling or unable to prevail in intraparty battles. In the Senate, by contrast, the greater proportion of the party that was internationalist, the more relaxed and staggered six-year election cycle, and the more individualistic rules of a smaller legislative body all allowed internationalists much greater power—despite the fact that Republican leadership was in unilateralist hands. As has been shown, therefore, whereas unilateralists in the House often held their party and the institution hostage to their extreme views, internationalists in the Senate time and again joined with Democrats to block unilateralist legislation pushed by their leaders or coming from the House. In fact, the history of Clinton vs. the unilateralists is an excellent example of what James Madison, the nation's fourth President, foresaw as the Senate's constitutional role: a "cool and deliberate" balance against "irregular passions."

Internationalist positions have been illustrated often in the preceding discussion of the unilateralists' clashes with the Clinton Administration. Although internationalists endorsed consolidation of foreign affairs agencies and ample appropriations for the U.S. military, they also supported adequate funding of the cooperative tools of statecraft, including foreign aid. By and large they were for aid to Mexico in the peso crisis, for funding of the IMF, for paying back dues to the UN in full, and against using Mexico City language to block these policies at home or gut population control programs overseas. Though skeptical of humanitarian interventions, internationalists generally supported the Administration's efforts to mediate foreign conflicts, and they voted for the troops needed to fulfill the Dayton peace accord on Bosnia, approved the air strikes on Kosovo, and endorsed the funding needed to back the North Korean Agreed Framework. They voted for the CWC and wanted desperately to postpone the vote on the CTBT rather than see it defeated, and they wanted a ballistic missile defense built within the context of a renegotiated ABM Treaty.

Given these views, Republican internationalists must have found the positions taken by the unilateralists almost as objectionable as the Clinton Administration did. As Senator Chuck Hagel (R-Nebr.) put it, "There has been a gross miscalculation by politicians—in my party mainly—that Americans are not interested" in world affairs, and a failure to understand that "we now live in an interconnected world. The Republican party—at least some elements of it—has been the last to recognize that." Caught between unilateralists' strength in their own party and an Administration often inattentive to foreign affairs or failing to inspire confidence, the problem of Republican internationalists has been the classic one of a minority within a majority: how to remain effective and still serve its convictions. As often as conscience would allow—on Taiwan, on Iraq, on military funding, even on the merits of the CTBT—internationalists voted with their leaders, and it was easy for them to join their unilateralist colleagues in opposing idealist positions. But at least as often they showed great courage by voting against their party and criticizing its failings. It has not been a comfortable position for them, but it has kept alive the possibility of a centrist Republican foreign policy.

4

The Prospects for
Bipartisan Statecraft

A FTER A HALF-DECADE struggle, the Clinton Administration
and the Republican majority in Congress appeared in their
last year to reach an exhausted *modus vivendi*. The Administration, for its part, had caved on foreign affairs agencies reorganization, the overthrow of Saddam Hussein and ballistic missile
defense, while the Republicans had funded the IMF and the
UN and let Clinton have his peacekeepers in Bosnia and
Kosovo. The chemical weapons convention was ratified while
the test ban treaty was killed.

Yet these outcomes represented accommodations to reality,
not a genuine meeting of minds. Unilateralists were forced to
fund foreign aid and international organizations by their lack of
votes in the Senate and Clinton's adroit use of budgetary
brinkmanship, while they acquiesced in various overseas interventions because of the President's powers as commander in

chief and their own determination to fund the military. Clinton, for his part, "accepted" reorganization, NMD and Iraqi liberation legislation only as last-ditch efforts to avoid losing control of those issues completely. Indeed, it was only on specific trade liberalization measures that Clinton and most Republicans really thought alike. Otherwise, the President's view of his opponents was expressed by his reaction to the CTBT defeat, which he called isolationist, a "reckless," irresponsible action by "hardline Republicans," and "partisan politics of the worst kind."

Partisanship

It *was* partisan, of course, but the record shows that the politics of American foreign policy in the post-cold-war era has been driven by more than mindless partisanship. While party affiliations continue to play a role, crossparty factional cooperation and intraparty factional struggles are now almost as common as partisan conflict. Equally important, although personal animosity is certainly at distressing levels, the contest remains very much a substantive one, powered by rival philosophies about how to deal with the new realities of the post-cold-war world.

Democratic *idealists* believe that the national interest now requires the projection of American values abroad virtually as much as their defense in America. However, Democratic *pragmatists* still give priority to helping the disadvantaged at home, while Republicans, especially *unilateralists*, limit the national interest to America's security and prosperity, as well as the preservation of the American way of life in the United States. *Unilateralist* Republicans have little faith in the efficacy of international cooperative enterprises, be they organizations, treaties or regimes, to defend key national interests; they also have little faith in cooperative tools of American statecraft like aid and diplomacy, preferring harder, coercive tools like armed force. Their *internationalist* colleagues, on the other hand, believe that cooperative efforts are good ways to lower costs and risks if properly used, while *Democrats* actually prefer multilateral tools for their consensus-building qualities. Indeed, *idealist* Democrats believe that new, post-cold-war threats to U.S. interests demand multilateral solutions, while *Republicans*, particularly *unilateralists*, often just don't believe in the new threats' importance, and in any case fear the multilateral cure far more than the transnational disease.

In some ways, the factional structure based on these differences makes partisanship less relevant to foreign policy outcomes. The centrist factions in each party—particularly the Republican internationalists—have far more in common with each other than with the extreme factions in their own parties. Certainly these moderate elements are what has enabled the parties to continue some cooperation with each other as they moved farther apart politically. Democratic pragmatism takes the ideological edges off Democratic idealism, softening the dilemma posed by the clash between the party's mission to uplift the disadvantaged and the limits of even a superpower's compassion. Republican internationalism similarly ameliorates the problem of an ideology that celebrates unfettered competition in an international system growing ever more linked and global; it relieves Republican conservatism of the stark choice

This cartoon first appeared in *The Christian Science Monitor* on December 18, 1998, and is reproduced with permission. ©1998 The Christian Science Publishing Society. All rights reserved.

between unilateral action and no action at all by using American leadership to bend multinational mechanisms toward national interests. Partisanship is also weakened by the fact that, on some issues, Republican unilateralists and Democratic idealists make common cause against the more moderate and centrist forces in both parties.

But though factionalism may encourage cooperation across party lines, partisanship can also be expected to continue to influence policy outcomes. For one thing, as long as government remains divided by party, partisan differences over domestic issues will inevitably spill over to heighten the inevitable constitutional struggle between the branches over foreign policy. Moreover, as argued at the outset, which foreign policy factions are dominant in each party will continue to be strongly influenced by which party controls which branch. Democrats tend to be idealist in Congress and pragmatist in the executive; Republicans are often unilateralist on the Hill but usually internationalist in the White House. If this is so, one can expect to see any future divided government pit a moderate executive against an ideological Congress—a situation like that in either the later years of the Clinton Administration (if the pattern of the late 1990s persists) or like that in the Bush Administration (if the sea changes of 1992 and 1994 are both reversed).

But one should note that White House centrism would be ranged against congressional extremism whether or not divided government persists. Should both branches be captured by the same party, however, policy outcomes would probably differ depending on which party wins. In the Democrats' case, one recalls the first two years under Clinton (1993–94), when congressional idealism swamped the new President's pragmatic instincts. Examples of unified Republican government are too far back in U.S. history to hold much relevance to post-cold-war circumstances, but there are reasons to believe that a Republican President would be better able than a Democrat to control his party's extremist faction. First, the two Democratic factions are not as ideologically distinct as their Republican counterparts. Pragmatists are just restrained idealists, making it harder for a

Democratic President to resist the pressure from his party's idealists in Congress. Second, as American "cowboy philosopher" Will Rogers pointed out years ago when he said, "I don't belong to any organized political party; I'm a Democrat," Republicans tend to be more disciplined. More senior Republican legislators are also used to working with a Republican in the White House, and for this reason also may be more likely to defer to presidential authority than their Democratic colleagues.

And the Winner . . .

Once elected, how likely are the presidential candidates in the 2000 elections to fit these predictions? Judging by their personal records, their campaign rhetoric and the kinds of foreign policy advisers they have chosen, it seems that George W. Bush is somewhat closer to the moderate faction of the Republican party than Al Gore is to Democratic centrists. Bush's "Vulcans," as the informal name given to his policy team implies, draw their experience at least as much from the Reagan as the Bush Administration, so one could expect from him a tougher approach than some Republican internationalists might favor. As far as one can tell from a candidate who has no foreign policy record, however, it would still probably be essentially internationalist; it was Reagan after all who reached epochal arms-control agreements with Mikhail Gorbachev's Soviet Union, championed democracy against authoritarian governments of the Right as well as the Left (including the ouster of Ferdinand Marcos from the Philippines and "Baby Doc" Duvalier from Haiti), and wound up supporting the UN as a key institution in international relations. Al Gore, on the other hand, seems slightly to the left of Bill Clinton in foreign policy. His well-known advocacy within the Administration (along with Madeleine Albright) of humanitarian and peacekeeping interventions overseas and his prominent views on such leading-edge environmental issues as global warming are two of the more obvious ways in which he leans toward the idealist approach, albeit from an essentially pragmatist position (for example, he continued to support free trade during the campaign in spite of his need for trade union support). Thus it seems likely that he would be somewhat less able to resist pressure from idealists in Congress than Bush would pressure from unilateralists.

Whatever the outcome in 2000, there are reasons to hope that factional partisanship will grow somewhat weaker over the long run. First, as the post-cold-war years lengthen, experience will tend to dilute ideology. Choices on many issues will have been made and their results known; there will be fewer abstractions in the policy universe to debate. Second, as long as prosperity lasts it will strengthen the political center, moderating attitudes on all issues and pushing party leaders toward cooperation. Finally, there is also the dark possibility that radical external events—a newly repressive and aggressive government in Russia, a global economic collapse, a terrorist attack in the United States—will reconcentrate the foreign policy mind, dramatically strengthening the role of external factors in policy outcomes.

Still, the differing views sketched above of national interests, threats to them, and appropriate means for responding to those threats will not soon disappear. Moreover, although expressions of radical conservatism in the Congress weakened during the 2000 campaign as Republicans reached toward centrist voters, marked differences between the presidential candidates on such domestic issues as tax cuts for the wealthy, privatization of social security, Medicare reform, abortion rights and gun control show that the political polarization of the parties continues. If one also assumes a continuation of post-cold-war turmoil with its high human costs as well as the relentless, technologically driven march of globalization and interdependence, then one also should expect that the parties' missions will continue to confront their members with stark foreign policy dilemmas. It is hard to escape the conclusion that the basics of the political system operating these past six years are therefore still very much in place, or that partisan factionalism will continue to influence the politics of American foreign policy for some years to come.

Talking It Over

A Note for Students and Discussion Groups

This issue of the HEADLINE SERIES, like its predecessors, is published for every serious reader, specialized or not, who takes an interest in the subject. Many of our readers will be in classrooms, seminars or community discussion groups. Particularly with them in mind, we present below some discussion questions—suggested as a starting point only—and references for further reading.

Discussion Questions

One of the tenets distinguishing unilateralists from centrists of both parties is their concept of the nature of today's international system. Is that system still essentially realist in nature, characterized by a survival-of-the fittest struggle for power and wealth? Or has the growing interdependence of nation-states, the globalization of their economies, and strengthening transnational links among their peoples created a fundamentally different, more cooperative system?

Democrats and Republicans often have very different ideas about the proper scope of foreign policy concerns. Should

American statecraft be restricted to tangible interests in security and prosperity? Or should the United States give as much or more prominence to its values as to its interests, seeking for example to enlarge the sphere of market democracy or relieve human suffering overseas?

Have serious threats to American interests disappeared since the end of the cold war? Do transnational concerns such as international crime, terrorism, global pollution and climate change, the spread of disease, the proliferation of weapons of mass destruction, population growth and the migration of people now require the kind of attention that the Soviet threat once received?

When it comes to the instruments of statecraft, need the United States rely on unilateral, even coercive measures? Can the United States entrust the nation's security to treaty promises and international organizations, or are the real threats such that *only* treaties and multilateral regimes can deal with them? Or, on the other hand, are the real threats not from abroad at all but here at home, demanding more attention and resources for domestic than foreign affairs?

Winston Churchill famously said that democracy is the worst form of government, except for all the others. Is partisan factionalism on foreign policy a sign of health in American government during a period of historic transition, or an indication that our democracy is failing in one of its major responsibilities?

Annotated Reading List

CQ Weekly Reports and yearly *Almanacs*. Washington, D.C., Congressional Quarterly, Inc., 1995-2000. The indispensable source of information on the complexities of congressional action.

Hamilton, Lee H., "The Role of Congress in Foreign Policy." Washington, D.C., Center for Strategic and International Studies, November 19, 1998. This distinguished former representative critiques Congress's inaction, overreaction, unilateralism, politicization and failure to take responsibility.

Huntington, Samuel, "The Erosion of American National Interests." *Foreign Affairs*, Sept./Oct. 1997. Argues that various commercial interests and ethnic groups have become so influential and divisive that a moratorium on foreign policy should be declared until cohesiveness returns.

Kitfield, James, "The Folk Who Live on the Hill." *The National Interest*, Winter 1999/2000. Explains unilateralist attitudes as a result of generational shift, leadership fatigue, foreign affairs ignorance and antigovernment fiscal attitudes, including on defense spending.

Lind, Michael, "Civil War by Other Means." *Foreign Affairs*, Sept./Oct. 1999. Describes the polarization of American politics along regional lines as the parties have become more geographically concentrated and politically extreme.

Luck, Edward C., *Mixed Messages: American Politics and International Organization, 1919-1999*. Washington, D.C., Brookings Institute, 1999. This in-depth treatment puts current issues between the United States and the United Nations in historical perspective and wonderful detail.

Rosner, Jeremy D., *The New Tug-of-War: Congress, the Executive Branch, and National Security*. Washington, D.C., Carnegie Endowment for International Peace, 1995. Its thesis is that presidential power in foreign affairs is a function of national danger, but detailed treatment of peacekeeping and aid to Russia shows that how the Administration does business is also critical to success.

Sloan, Stanley, Locke, Mary, and Yost, Casimir A., *The Foreign Policy Struggle: Congress and the President in the 1990s and Beyond*. Washington, D.C., Institute for the Study of Diplomacy, Georgetown University, 2000. This report of the Foreign Policy and Congress Discussion Group includes 10 case studies of legislative-executive interaction and resulting conclusions.

Zakheim, Dov S., *Congress and National Security in the Post-Cold War Era*. Washington, D.C., The Nixon Center, October 1998. More up-to-date than Rosner's book, this one suffers from being focused only on defense issues rather that broader foreign policy matters. It finds that Congress still generally follows the President on defense.

Online Resources

CENTER FOR STRATEGIC AND INTERNATIONAL STUDIES (CSIS), 1800 K St., NW, Washington, DC, 20006; (202) 887-0200; Fax (202) 775-3199 ▪ Founded in 1962, CSIS is a public policy research institution dedicated to analysis and policy impact. Its goal is to inform and shape selected policy decisions in government and the private sector. **www.csis.org**

CONGRESSIONAL QUARTERLY INC. (CQ), 1414 22nd St., NW, Washington, DC, 20037; (800) 432-2250 ▪ CQ aims to educate members of Congress and the general public about the most current issues in government, politics and public policy. Publishes *CQ Weekly*, *CQ Daily Monitor*, *CQ.com On Congress* and *CQ Press*. **www.cq.com**

INSTITUTE FOR FOREIGN POLICY ANALYSIS (IFPA), Central Plaza Building, 10th floor, 675 Massachusetts Ave., Cambridge, MA 02139; (617) 492-2116; Fax (617) 492-8242 ▪ Founded in 1976, IFPA is a nonprofit, nonpartisan research organization that examines national security, political economics and foreign policy issues confronting the United States **www.ifpa.org**

U.S. CONGRESS ▪ The website of the United States Congress provides links to House and Senate directories, congressional records and text and summaries of legislation. **www.congress.gov**

CLINTON
versus
THE UNILATERALISTS

CLINTON WINS

key Dayton troop votes in House (12/13/95)
CWC approved (4/28/97)
IMF funding approved (10/21/98)
key Kosovo war votes (4/28/99)
UN arrears payment (11/19/99)
House passes China PNTR (5/24/00)
Senate passes China PNTR (9/19/00)

CLINTON COMPROMISES

foreign affairs reorganization approved (10/21/98)
Iraq Liberation Act cleared by Senate (10/5/98)
BMD deployment approved (3/17/99)
BMD decision postponed (9/1/00)

CLINTON LOSSES

peso crisis aid (1/30/95)
Clinton pulls fast track (11/7/97)
Rep. Cox's nine China bills (11/6/97)
CTBT defeat (10/13/99)
House passes Taiwan Act (2/1/00)

Source: Terry L. Deibel

Editorial Advisory Committee

CHAIRMAN

Richard H. Ullman

David K.E. Bruce Professor of International Affairs, Center of International Studies, Princeton University

---

David B. H. Denoon

Professor of Politics and Economics, New York University

Rosalie W. Fitzpatrick

*Great Decisions Coordinator,
Georgia Council for International Visitors*

Christine R. Lucas

Development Coordinator for Leadership Florida, Tallahassee

Ponchitta A. Pierce

Television Host and Producer, FPA Director

Lawrence G. Potter

Deputy director of Gulf/2000, a research and documentation project on the Persian Gulf states, currently teaching at Columbia University

Thomas G. Weiss

Distinguished Professor of Political Science at The Graduate School and University Center of The City University of New York

Karen M. Rohan

FPA Editor in Chief, Ex officio

FPA's Editorial Advisory Committee members recommend ways of improving quality and outreach of publications and give direction on issues that should be addressed and the best authors to write about them.

CITIZEN'S GUIDE
TO
U.S. FOREIGN POLICY

by the Editors of the Foreign Policy Association

NONPARTISAN BRIEFS on nine key foreign policy issues facing the nation. Published quadrennially by FPA since 1968, the objective has been to raise the level of foreign policy debate. The guide has traditionally been endorsed by the chairmen of the Democratic National Committee and the Republican National Committee, as well as the president of the League of Women Voters of the United States.

2000 TOPICS: Globalization and trade • Russia • Middle East • Defense and security • China and Taiwan • Global environment • The United Nations • Latin America • Humanitarian intervention

Published July 2000.
ISBN: 0-87124-192-7
Product ID No. 31491
Price: $9.95, PLUS $2.50 POSTAGE AND HANDLING

FPA.org

At FPA online, you can:

➤ Find listings of current and past publications

➤ Take part in a discussion on foreign policy with other FPA members

➤ Get the latest updates to *Great Decisions* articles

➤ Download the Tips for Discussion Group Leaders booklet

➤ Read the results of FPA's latest annual National Opinion Ballot Report

➤ Use the Readings and Resources page to link directly to *Great Decisions* suggested readings

➤ Check out reference maps, designed especially for the web

➤ Get the latest information on Foreign Policy Association events and speakers

Visit FPA website today

GREAT DECISIONS 2001

WRITTEN BY EXPERTS, each of the eight topics in the 104-page Great Decisions 2001 briefing book places the thematic/geographic issue in historical context and provides background, current policies and alternative policy options. Photographs, maps, charts and editorial cartoons supplement the text. Annotated reading suggestions as well as additional resources, including websites, are included. An opinion ballot accompanies each topic so that readers can express their views.

GREAT DECISIONS 2001 TOPICS: U.S. Trade Policy • China and Taiwan • Missile Defense • U.S. and Iraq • International Health Crisis • Mexico Reexamined • European Integration • Conflict Resolution in Africa

Available January 2001, price: $12.00
ISBN no. 0-87124-194-3; product ID no. 31498

THE GREAT DECISIONS 2001 TEACHER'S GUIDE

Written by a master curriculum developer, the guide contains teaching strategies and activities, glossaries and reproducible handouts for each topic, for use in the classroom as well as discussion groups (44 pp.).

Available January 2001, price: $19.00
ISBN no. 0-87124-195-1; product ID no. 31499

HEADLINE SERIES, published since 1935, provides readers with concise, timely analysis of a specific area or issue in world affairs. These informative pocket-sized books are written by foreign policy experts, journalists and other authorities.

India: Old Civilization in a New World   HS 320
by Barbara Crossette, chief of *The New York Times* UN bureau, who previously served in South Asia as a correspondent for that newspaper. Published Spring 2000. (88 pp. $5.95)

The Japanese Economy at the Millennium: HS 319
Correspondents' Insightful Views
by Nicholas D. Kristof and Sheryl WuDunn of *The New York Times*, who wrote these thought-provoking articles on the Japanese economy for *The Times*. Published Fall 1999. (56 pp. $5.95)

Turkey Today: HS 317
Troubled Ally's Search for Identity
by Katherine A. Wilkens, former staff director of the Congressional House Foreign Affairs Subcommittee. Published Fall 1998. (80 pp. $5.95)

Right Makes Might: HS 316
Freedom and Power in the Information Age
by David C. Gompert, vice president of the RAND Corporation and director of its National Defense Research Institute. Published June 1998. (88 pp. $5.95)

The Persian Gulf in Transition   HS 315
by Lawrence G. Potter, deputy director of the Gulf/2000 Project and currently teaching international affairs at Columbia University. Published January 1998. (72 pp. $5.95)

The U.S. Role in the 21st Century World: HS 314
Toward a New Consensus?
by Stanley R. Sloan, senior specialist in international security policy for the Congressional Research Service, Library of Congress. Published October 1997. (64 pp. $5.95)